3-WIN SPONSORSHIP

3-WIN SPONSORSHIP

THE NEXT GENERATION OF SPORTS & ENTERTAINMENT MARKETING

JOHN R. BALKAM

NEW DEGREE PRESS

COPYRIGHT © 2019 JOHN R. BALKAM

3-WIN SPONSORSHIP

The Next Generation of Sports & Entertainment Marketing

ISBN   978-1-64137-337-1   *Paperback*

            978-1-64137-654-9   *Ebook*

CONTENTS

In loving memory of my grandparents—Robert and Laurin Balkam & Alfred and Esther Johnston.

INTRODUCTION

———

"Make a career of humanity. Commit yourself to the noble struggle for equal rights. You will make a better person of yourself, a greater nation of your country, and a finer world to live in."

—MARTIN LUTHER KING, JR.

**

In August 2017, Hurricane Harvey devastated Houston, Texas, to the tune of an estimated $125 billion worth of damage. The Category 4 hurricane took over 100 lives, displaced more than 30,000 people, and prompted more than 17,000 rescues. Harvey became tied with Hurricane Katrina as the costliest tropical cyclone on record and left most of the city of Houston under water.[1]

Not long after Hurricane Harvey ripped through Texas and Louisiana, a second massive hurricane hit the island of Puerto Rico in September 2017. Hurricane Maria was even more powerful than Hurricane Harvey leading up to its landfall in Puerto Rico—the Category 5 storm carried wind gusts of up to 175 miles per hour. Maria completely destroyed the islands of Dominica, Guadeloupe, and Martinique, and eventually flattened Puerto Rico, taking an estimated 3,057 lives and creating an island-wide blackout, which would not be fully fixed until roughly one year after the storm hit.[2]

Relief efforts began immediately, with help coming from government agencies, nonprofit organizations, and donors large and small across the United States. However, a great deal of aid came from an unlikely place: a big telecommunications company and a major professional sports league.

---

1   Lynch Baldwin, Sarah and David Begnaud. "Hurricane Maria Caused An Estimated 2,975 Deaths In Puerto Rico, New Study Finds". Aug. 28, 2018. *Cbsnews.Com.* (Accessed September 3, 2019).
2   2019. *Nhc.Noaa.Gov.* (Accessed September 3, 2019). https://www.nhc.noaa.gov/news/UpdatedCostliest.pdf.

HOME RUNS FOR HURRICANE RECOVERY

Major League Baseball's postseason takes place every year during October, and, in 2017, the start of the MLB playoffs coincided with the aftermath of hurricanes Harvey and Maria. MLB had ties to both Houston and Puerto Rico, as one of the top teams in baseball that year was the Houston Astros, and Houston's star player was Carlos Correa, a native of Puerto Rico.

As an official sponsor of Major League Baseball, T-Mobile felt compelled to use its platform and its resources to provide financial aid to those affected by the terrible hurricanes that year.

On October 6, 2017, T-Mobile announced that it would donate at least $1 million dollars for hurricane recovery to Team Rubicon, a nongovernmental organization founded by two Marines that unites the skills and experiences of military veterans with first responders to rapidly deploy emergency response teams.[3]

In addition, T-Mobile pledged to donate ten thousand dollars for every home run that was hit during the 2017 MLB postseason and created the #HR4HR (Home Runs for Hurricane Recovery), enabling fans to tweet out their support

---

3   "T-Mobile Announces #HR4HR Home Runs For Hurricane Recovery". 2017. *T-Mobile.Com*. Accessed September 3 2019.

for hurricane relief and trigger a one dollar donation from T-Mobile. T-Mobile eventually upped the ante during the World Series, pledging twenty thousand dollars for every home run and two dollars for every #HR4HR tweet.

At the time, T-Mobile President and CEO John Legere was quoted as saying, "Puerto Rico, Texas and Florida are home to some of the biggest baseball fans in the world, and they need our help. So we're stepping up. Plus, throughout the MLB Postseason, we're turning the biggest moments of the game into moments that really matter with every home run worth $10,000 — and every fan's tweet with #HR4HR adding to the relief effort."[4]

As the baseball playoffs ensued, a few incredible things happened. Number one, the Houston Astros, backed by their #HoustonStrong fan base and a talented young roster, advanced all the way to the World Series and defeated the Los Angeles Dodgers to win their franchise's first-ever MLB title. In addition, the ten teams that participated in that year's playoffs combined to set an MLB record for the most home runs hit in a single postseason with 104.

When the final tallies were all added up, T-Mobile's Home Runs for Hurricane Recovery produced a remarkable impact

---

4   Ibid.

for relief efforts from Harvey and Maria. In total, players, celebrities, and fans tweeted #HR4HR 776,000 times, racking up $1.5 million in donations. Combining both #HR4HR tweets and home runs, fans and players united to raise **more than $2,780,000** for Team Rubicon's Hurricane Recovery efforts.[5]

Through the #HR4HR campaign, T-Mobile, Major League Baseball, and fans showed that there's great power in sports and in sponsorship to positively impact communities in a time of need. It was simple, it was powerful, and it was driven by authentic engagement with the sport of baseball and its fans.

But in reflecting on the incredible outcomes of Home Runs for Hurricane Recovery, it occurred to me—why don't more corporate brands and sports and entertainment properties think about how they can combine doing good with building their brands and businesses?

The story of T-Mobile, Team Rubicon, and Major League Baseball teaming up for hurricane relief shows that the sports and entertainment world stands to drive *better business*

---

5   "Following Florence, T-Mobile Brings Back #HR4HR, Home Runs For Hurricane Recovery, For MLB Postseason". 2018. *T-Mobile.Com*. (Accessed October 6, 2019).

results when they commit to doing good and driving meaningful impact.

THE BIG PICTURE

The global sponsorship marketing industry is massive. Leading sponsorship evaluation and reporting agency, IEG, estimates that in 2018, sponsorship spending globally reached $65.8 billion. In North America, that number was an estimated $24.2 billion.[6]

Brands and properties involved in sponsorship deals grew at a rate of 4% between 2015 and 2018, according to IEG's sponsorship report.[7]

The sports and entertainment business has been growing so fast in recent years that one might excuse the leaders in the industry for thinking, "If it ain't broke, don't fix it." The companies, sports and entertainment properties, athletes, entertainers, artists, and marketers involved in making the industry go round have been making money hand over fist in the twenty-first century. More sports franchises are starting to become valued at greater than one billion dollars. Major League Baseball's best player, Mike Trout,

---

6   IEG. "What Sponsors Want & Where Dollars Will Go In 2018." Sponsorship.Com. (Accessed September 3, 2019).

7   Ibid.

signed a twelve-year, $426.5 million contract extension on March 24, 2019, securing the largest contract in sports history. Business is booming.

At the same time, though, are big-spending brands and rich sports teams getting a little too comfortable? Will the faucet of dollars continue to run for the foreseeable future for the top sports and entertainment properties in the world? Or are there some hurricane-like winds brewing from afar that will soon turn the sports and entertainment business upside down?

Consumers dictate the success of the sports, music, and movie industries, and, right now, consumers are more or less loving what they're getting. However, a large wave of "conscious consumers" are shaking up consumer-facing businesses all over the world. Consumers are expressing more and more that they want the companies they spend their money on to align with their personal values. That means being socially and environmentally responsible, and taking a big, bold stand on some of the biggest issues we face as a society today.

Some leaders in the sponsorship world might argue that they should "stick to sports" or "stick to entertainment." It's not a brand or an entertainment property's place to take a stand on an issue like gun violence or police brutality. In fact, doing so might ruffle enough feathers among its customer base that they might stop the gravy train in its tracks.

I believe the opposite is true. In order to continue the incredible growth and success of sports and entertainment as an industry, brands, teams, athletes, and entertainers should take a stand on social issues. They should communicate what they believe in. They should develop business practices that do no harm to the planet. They should emphasize diversity, equity, and inclusion in every touch point they have with their customers and employees.

I'm not naive enough to think that everyone will agree with me on this, but recent trends in the industry suggest that sports and entertainment-oriented organizations *should* take a stand on social and environmental issues if they want to continue to grow their businesses into the future. It seems that the twenty-first century consumer *demands* it.

WHY I WROTE THIS BOOK

In my professional career, my passion for the sports and entertainment industry has dovetailed with a sincere interest in social entrepreneurship. In studying and researching for this book, I came to realize that the business of sports, music, film, and creative work could be one that not only creates profits for investors, but also one that creates a great deal of value for the improvement of society and for the health of our planet.

That keen interest and the realization of this potential for social impact led me on a journey of learning and discovery. I interviewed over a dozen industry veterans, entrepreneurs, and leaders to get a better understanding of the current sports and entertainment marketing landscape and how it is evolving. I also dove into dozens of books, reports, case studies, and articles on purpose-driven marketing practices to help understand the best practices in the industry.

Not only that, but I also had the chance to learn by doing. For the past three years, I've had the opportunity to work at an intersection of sports, technology, education, and sponsorship marketing. Working on sponsorship deals with pro athletes, pro sports franchises, and major corporate brands helped me develop further understanding of how and why sponsorship deals are created.

This process of listening, reading, and doing has helped me learn about sponsorship on a deep level and synthesize those lessons into this book. If there is one thing I have taken away from this experience, it is that the sports and entertainment industry has an opportunity to positively impact millions of lives throughout the world.

THE CONVERSATION THAT SPARKED EVERYTHING

In the summer of 2018, I was starting my third year working at EVERFI in the Sports and Entertainment division. EVERFI is a leading education technology company building education for the real world to empower learners of all ages with the skills necessary to thrive in the twenty-first century. To do that, EVERFI creates partnerships in the private sector that enable companies and organizations to sponsor critical skills education, like financial literacy, health and well-being, and entrepreneurship. Powered by private sector resources, schools across the United States and Canada access their digital learning platform and course content at no cost.

Operating at the intersection of sports, sponsorship marketing, technology, and social impact, I began to see a trend. Major brands and sports properties had an appetite to both do good and do well through their sponsor partnerships.

Everything came to a head when having a conversation with a sponsorship professional working for a small agency in the Midwest, who I'll name Tyler for the purposes of this book.

A colleague and I had sat down for a meeting with Tyler in August 2018 and shared details about our company and how we worked together with leagues, teams, and brands to create meaningful, measurable social impact in the communities they care about.

Tyler stopped us in the middle of our presentation and told us, "This is really cool what you guys are doing. **Every sponsor and every team *wants* to make an impact on their community when they build a partnership, but it's often the *last thing* that gets thrown in at the end of a deal. Most of the time, both sides just say, 'Let's get the deal done and figure out the community portion later.'"**

Tyler's comment really struck me. It seemed to me that sponsorship professionals were missing a major opportunity. In effect, they were treating the social impact portion of deals like baseball general managers treat the "Player to be named later," in MLB trades. This perspective didn't make sense to me.

Given all of the intractable social issues we face in the United States and around the world, how could companies and sports franchises make social impact an afterthought in their partnership discussions?

Not only that, but given the mountains of consumer data that show people today expect the brands they purchase from to align with their social and environmental values, I felt perhaps the sports sponsorship world was at major risk of losing touch with today's "conscious consumer."

This experience provoked and inspired something in me that drives me each day. It inspired me to set out in search of the best examples in the sports and entertainment world of how brands, athletes, teams, and community organizations have teamed up to create meaningful impact on the environment, on youth, and on the communities they care about.

FROM "WIN-WIN" TO "WIN-WIN-WIN"

You are familiar with the concept of win-win deals, in which both sides in an agreement come to terms that create value for their organizations. In an ideal sponsorship world, every brand and every property create win-win sponsorships.

This book, however, is not about win-win sponsorships. This book aims to create a framework for win-win-win deals in the sponsorship marketing space. The "third win," in this case, is value created on behalf of the environment, on behalf of society at-large, or on behalf of the community being served by the brand and the property.

As consumer behavior continues to demand that companies, athletes, and teams take a stand on social and environmental issues, I believe "Three-Win Sponsorship" will become the norm, not the exception. Therefore, the sports and entertainment sponsorship world should have guideposts and templates to create these new types of deals.

Sponsorship professionals should keep doing sponsorship deals in a traditional, "win-win" way at their own risk. Consumer behaviors and attitudes around social and environmental issues have been changing rapidly, and sponsorship pros must keep up with the times.

Consumers appreciate when you take a stand on a social issue. Athletes such as Colin Kaepernick and Serena Williams have been leading the way in this area, but leading brands like Nike and T-Mobile have started to follow suit. Yes, you may rub some consumers the wrong way, but, on the whole, the majority of consumers will laud you for standing up for what you believe in, particularly if they believe in the same thing.

Younger generations that we've been calling the Millennial Generation and Gen Z have shown particular interest in new sports and entertainment offerings like eSports and have not necessarily shown interest in legacy pro sports leagues. Aligning with younger generations' values will be critical to winning over their hearts, minds, and wallets going forward.

SO WHAT?

Why does the Three-Win Sponsorship model matter? Why should you be thinking along these lines now and into the future?

By integrating a third win into partnerships, brands and properties will produce better business results than they would see from primarily focusing on the two wins in traditional sponsorship deals.

You don't need to take my word for it, either: the top brands, teams, athletes, and entertainers are *already doing this*, and it is helping them win and retain customers. There are so many stories from across the sports and entertainment world of successful Three-Win sponsorship deals, and I've been fortunate to uncover several of them and speak with a number of the people responsible for building them.

I hope your takeaway from this book is this: when you combine sponsorship affiliation with a beloved team, athlete, or entertainer, and authentic social good and community engagement, brands can amplify the outcomes they are looking for from a business perspective.

I wrote this book for practitioners—the teams and individuals behind the multibillion-dollar sponsorship industry across the world. The examples, frameworks, and case studies in this book are written with you in mind because you are the ones who will get to decide how the industry adjusts to changing consumer behavior.

However, as I've moved along this journey of discovery and learning about the power of Three-Win Sponsorship, I have come to believe that any brand leader could benefit from learning the principles I will outline in this book.

WHAT TO EXPECT FROM THIS BOOK

Three-Win Sponsorship will break down into the following structure. In Part One, we will explore the origins of sponsorship as we know it today by telling the story of Arnold Palmer and Mark McCormack, and how their partnership effectively birthed the sports marketing industry. Plus, we'll look at the 1984 Olympic Games in Los Angeles and how ambitious and visionary leaders saved the Olympic movement by, in effect, inventing modern corporate sponsorship. We will also examine how, at the very beginning, sponsorship and social good were directly tied together.

We will then dig into how sponsorship marketing has evolved from simply producing brand awareness to where it is today, with sophisticated activations and intricate social media campaigns. Readers will get a solid foundation on the four phases of modern sponsorship in order to understand how Three-Win sponsorships are ushering in a new era of sponsorship.

To round out Part One, we will examine the rise of the "conscious consumer" so that readers might fully understand what motivates today's consumers and fans. We will look at some leading research and survey data to emphasize the ramifications of this movement on our businesses.

In Part Two, we will dig into the five core principles I've uncovered that make up a successful Three-Win sponsorship. For each principle, we will look at stories from leading brands, talent, and properties that have exemplified the right way to both do good and do well through sponsorship.

A few examples that we'll explore in this book include:

- How Super Bowl 50 became the most giving, most sustainable, most attended, and most diverse Super Bowl ever.
- Why US Bank decided to tear up its old sponsorship strategy and move toward completely aligning its sponsorship portfolio with its community engagement platform.
- How the University of Colorado Boulder's Athletic Department became the most sustainable department on campus, sparked a "green" movement across the entire Pac-12 Conference, and how it found ways to attract corporate sponsorship and amplify sustainable behaviors among its fan bases.

- Why Anheuser-Busch completely changed the way that its measures the success of its sponsorships and compensates its sponsor partners.
- In what ways Nike's thirtieth-anniversary "Just Do It" campaign exemplified the need to be authentic and stand up for the values of the company and the athletes it partners with.

Finally, in Part 3, we will explore the question, "What role do I have to play in the shift towards Three-Win sponsorship?"

We will attempt to answer this question from the perspective of talent, properties, and brands in order to make the principles actionable for all players involved in sponsorship marketing.

**

At the first-annual Laureus World Sports Awards in 2000, former South African President Nelson Mandela presented the Lifetime Achievement Award to legendary Brazilian soccer star, Pele.

In his opening speech, Mandela shared a message that has inspired millions of athletes and sports fans across the world ever since:

"Sport has the power to change the world. It has the power to inspire. It has the power to unite people in a way that little else does. It speaks to youth in a language they understand. Sport can create hope where once there was only despair. It is more powerful than government in breaking down racial barriers. It laughs in the face of all types of discrimination."

Keeping Mandela's words in mind, let's embrace the platform we have in the sports and entertainment world. Let's attack the biggest, most difficult social and environmental issues of our time with enthusiasm and creativity. Let's reinvent how we do business. Let's truly change the world.

PART ONE

A BRIEF HISTORY OF MODERN SPONSORSHIP

CHAPTER 1

THE ORIGINS OF MODERN SPONSORSHIP

———

"If somehow, we have brought the world just a little closer together, perhaps we have secured a better future for the children of the world."

—PETER UEBERROTH

**

Sponsorship as a marketing discipline is still relatively new, so we don't have to look too far back in the history books to find the key individuals and events that made sponsorship an industry that is worth more than $60 billion today.

Let's look at how one exceptional professional athlete became the father of celebrity endorsements, and after that we'll dive into how one major sporting event became an inflection point for the entire sports and entertainment marketing industry.

"THE KING" AND "THE FATHER OF SPORTS MARKETING"

Arnold Palmer was one of the most accomplished professional golfers of all time—consistently in the conversation with a handful of greats like Jack Nicklaus, Gary Player, and Tiger Woods. But it was what Palmer accomplished in the business world that changed the sports industry forever.

In the prime of his career during the 1950s and 1960s, Palmer won seven major championships, including the most prestigious tournament in golf, The Masters, four times. Nicknamed "The King," Palmer was renowned for his kindness and grace with fans as much as for his success in tournament golf.

He built such an adoring fan base that they gave themselves a nickname—"Arnie's Army"—and religiously followed Palmer around the golf course because of their admiration for the man and for his aggressive, swashbuckling golf game. Over time, he became a globally recognized brand due to his partnership with a pioneering businessman.

In 1958, Palmer was approached by a lawyer from Cleveland named Mark McCormack about the possibility of McCormack representing Palmer as his business manager focused on marketing and endorsements. McCormack was a huge golf fan who had become disenchanted with his work in corporate law. He was described as having "two loves: golf and making money," and he was determined to find a way to combine the two of them.[8]

At this point in time, professional athletes were not multi-millionaires. In fact, even the elite golfers on the Professional Golfers' Association (PGA) Tour were scraping by on their winnings from tournaments and constantly searching for additional sources of income off the course.

McCormack was puzzled by this situation. He thought, "Pro athletes are adored and have a unique skill set. Why didn't they make more money?" He felt like there was a huge opportunity to represent pro golfers to create advertising partnerships with corporate brands and take a small percentage of their earnings.[9]

---

8   Futterman, Matthew. *Players: The Story of Sports and Money, and the Visionaries Who Fought to Create a Revolution.* Simon & Schuster, 2016.

9   Ibid.

And so, after a courtship of a few years, Palmer and McCormack came to an agreement starting fall 1959 that would set the foundation for a firm called International Management Group (IMG). Palmer became the key client for what turned out to be perhaps the most influential firm in sports marketing history.

As his long stretch of golf excellence began to decline in the 1960s, Palmer worked closely with McCormack to become a celebrity endorser of commercial products. McCormack secured deals for Palmer to endorse Golf Magazine, United Airlines, Bausch & Lomb, and eventually over fifty different products.

"He was the pioneer," said Bob Williams, CEO and COO at Burns Entertainment & Sports Marketing, which represents brands who hire celebrities for endorsements. "He was the first celebrity in the sports world to have a marketing agent."[10]

"He established the sports marketing industry as we knew it," Alastair Johnston, Palmer's longtime agent at IMG told The New York Times. "It became a much more sophisticated exercise. It became a real business with real money."[11]

---

10 Gelles, David. *"Golf Great Arnold Palmer Was Also a Pioneering Pitchman."* The New York Times, Sept. 26, 2016. (9/24/2019)

11 Ibid.

Arnold Palmer's prolific golf game turned into an even more prolific and lengthy career as a pitchman. It is estimated that Palmer earned $875 million over the course of his life through endorsements, appearances, licensing, and golf course design, according to Forbes.[12]

"What he did, creating a brand unto himself, was the blueprint for everyone who came after him, whether it be LeBron, or Jordan or Tiger Woods," said Matthew Futterman, author of *Players: The Story of Sports and Money, and the Visionaries Who Fought to Create a Revolution.*[13]

With all of that financial success, Arnold Palmer was also able to be a renowned philanthropist. In 1959, Palmer and his wife Winnie created a charitable foundation dedicated to positively impacting and empowering children and strengthening communities by investing in health, wellness, and the environment.

To this day, Arnie's Army Charitable Foundation operates out of Orlando, Florida, pursuing the mission of "The King"

12 Badenhausen, Kurt. "How Arnold Palmer Earned $875 Million During Legendary Career In Golf." *Forbes SportsMoney,* September 26, 2019. (Accessed September 24, 2019).

13 Gelles, David. *"Golf Great Arnold Palmer Was Also a Pioneering Pitchman." The New York Times,* Sept. 26, 2016. (Accessed September 24, 2019).

and further cementing Palmer's legacy as an athlete who was bigger than sports.

Not only did Arnold Palmer create the template for the athlete as a major endorser of corporate products, but he also showed pro athletes for generations to come that they could use their platforms for good.

**

In the twenty-first century, the Olympic Games have become one of the largest events on the sports and entertainment calendar. According to Forbes, the 2018 Winter Olympics in Pyeongchang, South Korea, cost an estimated $12.9 billion to put on, and reached five billion people worldwide through television broadcast. NBC has already committed $7.65 billion for the broadcast rights to the Olympics from 2021 to 2032.[14]

Why have the Olympics become such big business? For one thing, the global nature of the games ensures advertisers will have access to some of the biggest audiences they could possibly reach during any one event. Plus, given that the games are put on once every four years, an element of scarcity adds to the stakes of the event and makes people around the world

14 Settimi, Christina. "*By The Numbers: The 2018 Pyeongchang Winter Olympics*". Aug. 8, 2018. *Forbes.Com*. (Accessed September 24, 2019).

pay attention. Add in the fact that the athletes are competing *for their home nations,* and *for their fellow country men and women,* and you have a recipe for a popular event.

Legendary Australian swimmer Dawn Fraser has said of the games, "The Olympics remain the most compelling search for excellence that exists in sport, and maybe in life itself." There is something about that search for excellence that draws human beings in, that inspires us, that moves our emotions, and leaves an indelible impact on us.

Massive global audiences. High stakes competition. National pride. Exemplary human performances. In many ways, these characteristics make the Olympic Games a perfect platform for brands to latch on to, associate with, and advertise to consumers. The games are a perfect place to run large-scale sponsorship platforms. However, when we look at the history of the Olympics, this ideal marketing situation was not always the case.

LA84 SAVES THE OLYMPICS

During the 1970s, the Olympics were not in great shape. The 1972 Munich Games included an infamous hostage crisis. The '76 Montreal Games were a financial disaster in which the host city lost $1.5 billion. The 1980 Moscow Games were boycotted by over sixty countries.

The Olympic Games movement was in deep peril. But everything changed in 1984, and it set the stage for an explosion of growth in advertising that has carried us up to the present day.

When it came time for the International Olympic Committee (IOC) to decide on a host city for the 1984 Olympic Games, very few cities had even submitted a bid. City leaders around the globe had a hard time selling their constituents on an event that had been riddled with financial loss, political turmoil, and terrorism.

Only Los Angeles and Tehran had made legitimate bids for the '84 Games, but Tehran ultimately withdrew its bid, making Los Angeles the host city, almost by default.

The Los Angeles Organizing Olympic Committee (LAOOC), led by its CEO Peter Ueberroth, had unique challenges in organizing these games. For one, because the United States had boycotted the 1980 games in Moscow, Los Angeles could count on very little support from the IOC and the international Olympic family. Indeed, Russia countered with their own boycott of the 1984 games, refusing to send some of the world's most dominant athletes to compete in the United States during the middle of the Cold War.

At the same time, Los Angeles voters passed an amendment that prohibited the expenditure of government funds to fund the Olympics, leaving the LAOOC to shoulder the entire financial burden for organizing the '84 Summer Olympics. According to a story in CSQ magazine on Peter Ueberroth and these games, the LA Olympics "were to be the first, and only, privately financed Olympic Games in modern-day history. Not one penny was received in donations."[15]

Peter Ueberroth was the right man for this seemingly impossible job. A successful entrepreneur, Ueberroth had just sold the company he had founded, First Travel, for a significant sum to become the CEO of the LAOOC. During the 1960s, he had moved his family to the San Fernando Valley because he yearned to be his own boss, and "follow the entrepreneurial startup path."[16]

"I opened the first bank account [for the 1984 Olympics] with my own money," Ueberroth said. "We inched our way along."[17]

Ueberroth took on significant risk, like start-up company founders often do. Finding new and different ways to fund

---

15 Davis, David. "Peter Ueberroth: Showing Us The Gold Standard | CSQ Magazine". 2017. *CSQ | Magazine, Events, Community.* Accessed September 24 2019.

16 Ibid.

17 Ibid.

the Olympics seemed much like the challenge of building a company from scratch. By utilizing a very lean operation, with as few employees as possible and help from thousands of volunteers, Ueberroth and the LAOOC were able to avoid the pitfalls that doomed previous Olympics, like Montreal in 1976. Rather than investing hundreds of millions of dollars to build new facilities and stadiums, the LAOOC signed leases with existing facilities like The Forum, The Sports Arena, and the Los Angeles Memorial Coliseum.

LA did end up building two facilities—a swim center and a "velodrome" for cycling events— however, they were able to offset much of the cost through corporate sponsorship and media broadcasting rights.

The first big domino to fall for Ueberroth and his LA84 team was their successful negotiation with ABC-TV, selling the exclusive television broadcasting rights for $225 million, which was, at the time, a record deal. The ABC deal served as seed funding to operate the LA84 team's operations, and, from there, they set out to attract other corporations to affiliate with the games for a price.

Sponsorship was a relatively novel concept in the 1980s, a time in which radio and print advertising still ruled the day. However, Ueberroth realized he could create competition for marketing and advertising during the Olympics through creation of a so-called "golden circle" of Olympic sponsors. In this model, an exclusive group of a small number of companies would become "official sponsors" in different product categories, and a bidding war would ensue. Therefore, Burger King and McDonald's had to compete for the title of "official burger of the Olympics," a competition McDonald's won.

Soon, companies including Coca-Cola, Fuji Photo Film, and Converse were committing upwards of $14 million each to become the "official soft drink of the Olympics," or the "official athletic shoe of the Games." The category sponsorships that we've come to be very familiar within the sports and entertainment space can trace their origins to the success of the LA84 team.

Ueberroth and company secured an additional $126 million from sponsorship deals and ended up creating a surplus of $232.5 million once the games were all said and done. It was the most profitable sporting event in history.

The legacy of the 1984 Summer Olympic Games did not stop there. The LA84 Foundation was created and endowed with about forty percent of the profits from the games, roughly $93 million. It still operates to this day, and over the past thirty-five years it has impacted more than three million youth and families and supported over 2,200 nonprofit organizations, including the Boys and Girls Clubs of America,

KEEN Los Angeles, the YMCA, and the Professional Golfers Association of America Foundation.

**

As you can see, from the stories of the late Arnold Palmer, and the success of the '84 Olympics, doing good has been tied directly to doing well from the very beginning of modern sponsorship. If not for the tremendous success of Peter Ueberroth and his team of Olympic organizers, the Olympic movement may have fizzled out in the mid '80s. The creative marketing minds on the LA84 team also opened up a brand-new era of sponsorship marketing.

Almost immediately after the completion of the '84 Olympics, Peter Ueberroth was named the commissioner of Major League Baseball. From that position, Ueberroth applied many of the same principles his LA84 team used to attract big advertising and marketing spends for sponsorship of Major League Baseball. The sponsorship landscape had changed forever, and soon, every league, every team, and all of the elite athletes in pro sports were following the trend of "official sponsorship" categories.

The LA84 Olympics were a success beyond anyone's wildest dreams. Shrewd business management and operations of the '84 games led to a massive surplus, which was then able to seed a foundation dedicated to the support of youth sports development in Los Angeles and across the country.

LA84 was not only the gold standard for the planning and execution of a major sporting event, but it appears to have set a standard for what is possible when funds are set aside for social good and empowerment.

However, LA84's success brings up the question: where along the way did we forget about the social impact element of sponsorship that was embedded into the success of the '84 games? Was it an aberration, or was it ahead of its time?

THREE WINS FROM CHAPTER 1

1. Arnold Palmer was the pioneer of the professional athlete as pitchman archetype that we are so familiar with today. His work with Mark McCormack and IEG laid the foundation for athletes like Michael Jordan, Tiger Woods, and LeBron James to become the highest-paid celebrity endorsers in the world.

2. Likewise, Peter Ueberroth and the LA84 Olympics Games revolutionized sports and entertainment marketing from the property side. Ueberroth's creation of "category sponsorship" sparked an incredible growth of sponsorship spending in the '80s and '90s that continues to this day.

3. Not only were Palmer and Ueberroth pioneering figures in the sports and entertainment marketing industry, but they set the example for how social impact could be tied directly to sponsorship. They leveraged their tremendous financial success into an opportunity to fund charitable initiatives which have impacted millions of lives over the years.

CHAPTER 2

THE FOUR PHASES OF MODERN SPONSORSHIP

———

*"The target markets get the third win and it's **the most important win of all**. Best practice sponsors know that the most important connection in the equation is the connection between their brand and the target markets."*

—KIM SKILDUM-REID, AUTHOR AND

FOUNDER OF POWER SPONSORSHIP

**

While many sponsorship deals came before the 1984 Summer Games, the success of those games served as an inflection point for an explosion in sponsorship spending throughout the '80s, '90s and 2000s.

With increased marketing spend and the attention of executive leadership, sponsorship has become much more sophisticated over the last thirty-five years. Core to the evolution of sponsorship has been a shift from a focus on the sponsor and sponsee's needs to a focus on the target market's needs.

To understand why that shift has occurred, let's take a look at the evolution of modern sponsorship marketing, which we'll break down into four phases: awareness, activation, content, and purpose.

THE AWARENESS PHASE (1980S—MID-1990S)

The first phase of modern sponsorship marketing, which took place in the '80s and '90s, was all about exposure and **awareness**.

During this era, there was very little science to the way brands and properties did sponsorship deals, but, for the most part, sponsorship was all about slapping a company's logo on a billboard so that fans could become aware of that company's affiliation with their favorite team or sport.

I spoke with Georgetown University adjunct professor of sports industry management Marty Conway, and he told me that in the years following the 1984 Summer Olympics in Los Angeles, Peter Ueberroth's influence continued to spread throughout the rest of the sports industry.

As we mentioned in Chapter 1, Ueberroth was named commissioner of Major League Baseball shortly after the '84 Olympics, and one of the first things he did was apply the category sponsorship model he had pioneered at those Olympic games to baseball. Professor Conway worked for the Baltimore Orioles as the vice president of marketing and corporate partnerships from 1985 to 1992 and then for the Texas Rangers as vice president of marketing and communication. He told me this time period was the "golden era of official sponsorship."

Professor Conway said that every team and every league started going very hard after major companies to sell them on being the "official sponsor" of categories such as automotive, soft drink, and bank, for their property. For the most part, companies started buying in and putting their marketing dollars behind these teams. In reality, no property and no brand could really measure the return on investment of these sponsorships.

Kim Skildum-Reid is the author of *The Corporate Sponsorship Toolkit* and the founder of Power Sponsorship, a consulting agency that advises major corporate sponsors across the globe. Skildum-Reid has twenty-nine years' experience in corporate sponsorship and is one of very few professionals credited with defining and setting the best practice benchmark for the sponsorship industry. She is one of the sponsorship industry's foremost thought leaders.

In her 2012 book *The Corporate Sponsorship Toolkit*, Skildum-Reid describes the Awareness phase of sponsorship as "First Generation" sponsorship. She describes "First Generation" sponsorship as being "driven by gaining exposure and awareness, with a big dose of chief executive's choice thrown in for good measure," in the time leading up to and after the '84 Olympics.[18]

Skildum-Reid reflected that during this generation of sponsorship, "the focus was very clearly on sales, with immediate gains the driving force. Long-term benefits were rarely sought or even considered in this formula-based era."

Corporate brands paid very little attention to the key performance indicators for their businesses during the awareness era of sponsorship. There was a lot of room

---

18   Skildum-Reid, Kim. *The Corporate Sponsorship Toolkit: Using sponsorship to help people fall in love with your brand.* Freya Press, 2012.

for growth and improvement after this infancy stage, but sponsorship as a marketing tool started to become much more popular.

THE ACTIVATION PHASE (1990s–2000s)

As brands started to get wiser about their sponsorship portfolios, they began asking for more out of their property partners. They wanted to connect in a more personal, memorable way with consumers than just billboards inside of stadiums and arenas.

GMR Marketing's vice president of global sponsorship consulting Ania Sponaski describes this second iteration of modern sponsorship as being the **activation** phase.

As we moved into the late '90s and early 2000s, brands and properties began creating in-person experiences and events for fans that enabled them to see, taste, touch, smell, and hear the sponsor's products. At this time, brands hoped that by "activating" their affiliation with pro sports teams through fun and exciting experiences, they could increase their brand and product preference with those fans.

Activation, or leverage, of a sponsorship is what you do with the rights you gain as the sponsor of a property. It is the lounge or common area where you greet fans at the stadium;

it is the free beer that you get after running a road race; it is the silly game or giveaway that teams play on the big screen to engage with fans during a stoppage in play. Activation enables a brand to create connections with their target markets through experiences.

Professor Conway used an analogy to describe this phase of sponsorship: "If you are buying a sponsorship, it's basically like buying a flashlight. In order to use your flashlight, however, you have to put batteries in it to activate it, and make it work. That is what was happening here."

Conway went on to describe Pepsi's relationship with the NFL to reinforce the analogy. Pepsi was the official soft drink of the NFL, but they began activating that partnership through the Super Bowl Halftime Show, a time in which hundreds of millions of viewers have their eyeballs glued to their television screens.

Still, even with the integration of sponsorship activation into brand and property partnerships, it was very difficult to attribute these events and experiences to consumer purchases of sponsor products. Marketing executives all over the world were still unable to determine with true clarity what the return on investment (ROI) was for their sponsorship portfolios.

THE CONTENT PHASE (MID-2000S–MID-2010S)

In the mid-2000s, social media platforms such as Facebook and Twitter exploded onto the scene. Suddenly, consumers were flocking into these virtual town halls to tweet, comment, like, post, and scroll through content coming from friends, peers, and even strangers.

The social media boom made a significant influence on the sponsorship industry because companies, sports teams, musicians, artists, and other entertainment entities realized the power of connecting with their consumers and fans directly on digital media platforms.

Not only did it give marketers a way to speak directly with their customers, but it also enabled them to capture mountains of data on consumers' personal information, demographics, and preferences. Plus, Facebook, Twitter, and other platforms built more and more features onto their platforms, which enabled an unprecedented level of measurement for marketers wanting to understand the effectiveness of their advertising.

Content became king, and thus it ushered in the **content** phase of sponsorship. Brands and properties had to rewrite their sponsor partnerships to include nontraditional assets such as Facebook or Twitter posts. Social media experts had to be hired onto marketing teams all over the industry, and content creation became a massive priority for everyone involved in sponsorship.

Finally, big sponsorship spenders had a better way to measure their return on investment. The digital nature of social media empowered sponsors and properties to capture views, followers, engagements, and even create some attribution models to peg an ROI number to their spend.

Take the T-Mobile Home Runs for Hurricane Recovery campaign as an example. Throughout the 2017 MLB Playoffs, fans used the #HR4HR over 750,000 times to support the victims of Hurricanes in Houston, Florida, and Puerto Rico. Both T-Mobile and Major League Baseball embraced the power of content creation to engage with fans and put their platforms to good use in service of hurricane recovery efforts.

This focus on content and activation together has produced a major step up in effectiveness for sponsors. Skildum-Reid agrees: "Brand needs, integration and the achievement of multiple marketing objectives are drivers of this generation."[19]

---

19   Ibid.

THE PURPOSE PHASE (2010S–PRESENT)

What we have seen in the 2010s is a shift into the **purpose** phase of sponsorship, which is what this book is all about. More and more, leading sponsors are integrating social, political, and environmental causes into their sponsorship activation with teams, athletes, artists, and musicians. This enables companies to align with the personal values of their core audience and connect in a more meaningful way.

Sponsorship professionals continue to leverage all of the assets they've been using over the past thirty-five years, but sponsorship has come a long way from simply slapping a logo on a billboard. Today, brands and properties are constantly creating content to serve up to consumers in such a way that it feels personal to each viewer. Every company must create meaningful, authentic, engaging content to win over consumers hearts, minds, and ultimately their wallets.

Professor Conway told me that he sees sponsors measuring sponsorship not only for their return on investment or return on objectives, but also for a "return on heart," so to speak. In order to connect on an emotional level with today's consumer, purpose and cause marketing has become a driving force to successful sponsorship.

Skildum-Reid believes that in the twenty-first century, best-practice sponsorship "is about nurturing a brand's connection with a target market by putting their needs first."

"The number one concept that drives best practice...sponsorship is the idea of win-win-win," Skildum-Reid writes. "For years, good sponsorship was defined as being win-win, that is, the sponsor wins and the sponsorship seeker wins. While having this kind of mutual benefit is a great idea, this approach completely left out the most important part of the equation: The target markets."[20]

"Given that the target markets are the pivot point for the well-being of both the brand and the property, it makes perfect sense to make the target markets' needs and wants part of the basic infrastructure of best practice sponsorship."[21]

The third win, therefore, should be *the number one priority of all sponsors and sponsorship seekers*. Building and executing effective sponsorships today is no longer about making the CEO feel good by slapping his company's logo on a billboard at the ballpark. Best-in-class sponsorships are about creating value for the target audience in an authentic, meaningful way.

---

20 Ibid.
21 Ibid.

For that reason, we need to understand today's consumer a lot better. What does today's consumer value? What are their needs? How are they different from consumers in years past?

In the next chapter, we'll dive into how a new type of consumer will define sponsorship for years to come.

THREE WINS FROM CHAPTER 2

1. Sponsorship as a marketing discipline has evolved over the years. We can break down its evolution into four phases: **awareness**, **activation**, **content**, and **purpose.**
2. With each phase of modern sponsorship, an additional layer of sophistication has been added on to the marketing practices that came before. For example, from the awareness phase to the activation phase, sponsors sought more than just their logo on a billboard. They required their partners to provide signage and a means of leveraging their sponsorship through an event or through an in-game activation.
3. We are in the midst of a shift into the **purpose** phase of sponsorship. To build successful sponsorship deals, brands must take into account the value they are bringing to their target markets—the "third win." As sponsorship expert Kim Skildum-Reid has talked about, in this new era, the third win is the most important win of all.

CHAPTER 3

RISE OF THE CONSCIOUS CONSUMER

———

"People want – and are demanding – that companies do good in both words and deeds. Now more companies than ever have the means to actualize this. A cocktail of consumer desires, technology, and changing culture has made doing good both a practical reality and a new requirement for corporate survival across industries."

—ANNE BAHR THOMPSON, AUTHOR OF *DO GOOD: EMBRACING BRAND CITIZENSHIP TO FUEL BOTH PURPOSE AND PROFIT*

**

Sponsorship marketing has clearly evolved over the past thirty-five years, and that evolution has been driven by consumer desires and behaviors. It's no longer just about slapping a logo on a billboard because it won't move consumers' attitudes or behaviors whatsoever.

Today's twenty-first-century consumer is more powerful than the consumer watching the Summer Olympics on a no-definition TV back in 1984. The consumer in 2019 has technological tools including search engines, rating websites, and social media that have enabled them to do tons of research and due diligence on a brand before making a purchase.

The overarching trend in consumer behavior has been that consumers don't just purchase for the utility of the product: they purchase for the utility *and* the emotional fulfillment of the product. They are buying products that reinforce their own personal identity, values, and beliefs. This trend has important implications for marketers because you need to understand it when sourcing, buying, selling, and executing your sponsorships.

To better understand this paradigm, let's look at one of the most recognizable retail brands in the United States and how consumer behavior has shifted the way it positions its brand and its messaging.

GILLETTE'S TAGLINE GETS A FACELIFT

In February 1989, Gillette launched a new tagline in a sixty-second commercial that aired during the Super Bowl. The Procter & Gamble men's disposable razor brand put out this aspirational spot by depicting men thriving in various scenarios in their lives: on the playing field, in the meeting room, with their children, and in meeting—and presumably wooing—beautiful women. "Gillette—The Best a Man Can Get," the ad exclaimed in the form of an '80s jingle.

"The Best a Man Can Get" served as Gillette's mantra and brand identity for thirty years, positioning its razors as the premium choice for men. Then suddenly, in early 2019, the tagline was given a face lift with a twenty-first-century point of view.

"Is this the best a man can get?" asks a voiceover in Gillette's advertisement launched on January 14, 2019[22], while men are shown looking in the mirror, contemplating topics such as toxic masculinity, bullying, sexual harassment, and the #MeToo movement. The ad shows boys chasing or fighting with other boys and men standing around doing nothing. "Boys will be boys," says one man after another, as if they have been brainwashed into thinking that type of behavior was OK.

---

22   Gillette® 2019. "The Best Men Can Be." *Gillette.Com*. Accessed September 30, 2019.

The mood shifts, as a clip shows actor, activist, and P&G pitchman Terry Crews testifying during a hearing for the Sexual Assault Survivors' Rights Act saying, "Men need to hold other men accountable."

A narrator delivers the core message of the advertisement.

<quote>"Bullying is a problem; we can't hide from it. Sexual harassment is taking over—it's been going on for far too long. We can't laugh it off, making the same old excuses. But something finally changed. And there will be no going back. Because we….We believe in the best in men. To say the right thing. To act the right way. Some already are, in ways big and small. But some is not enough. Because the boys watching today will be the men of tomorrow."</quote>

"It's only by challenging ourselves to do more that we can get closer to our best," the spot concludes.

Gillette's new ad coincided with the launch of a social responsibility campaign called "The Best Men Can Be," focused on promoting "positive, attainable, inclusive and healthy versions of what it means to be a man." As part of the campaign, Gillette committed $1 million per year over three years to "non-profit organizations executing the most interesting and impactful programs designed to **help men of all ages achieve their personal best,"** according to the brand's website. Their first beneficiary was the Boys & Girls Clubs of America.[23]

Pankaj Bhalla, the North American brand director for Gillette, told The Atlantic magazine, "The intention was not to be political at all." Instead, Bhalla cited pressure from Millennial and Gen Z shoppers for the shift towards socially conscious advertising. "I think it is important to stand for more than the product's benefit that you provide, and I think that's the expectation of our younger audiences," Bhalla said.[24]

But why were Millennial and Gen Z shoppers putting brands to the test from a social ethics and values standpoint? Peggy Simcic Brønn, a professor of communication and culture at the Norwegian School of Management, Oslo who has tracked social responsibility marketing for more than two decades, suggested to The Atlantic that a decrease in trust in public institutions has left a void that younger consumers are expecting brands to fill. "NGOs and governmental institutions, which we depend on to address bad things, they're not doing it. So who's left to do it? That's business," said Brønn.[25]

---

23 "The Best Men Can Be | Gillette®". 2019. *Gillette.Com*. (Accessed September 30, 2019.)

24 Mull, Amanda. "Millennials Stare Into The Void, And Gillette Stares Back". *The Atlantic*. January 6th, 2019. (Accessed September 30, 2019.)

25 Ibid.

The Atlantic concluded that what these marketing efforts have helped to do is to rebrand capitalism in a time when young people are questioning its efficacy. "If we want the world to survive, we have to think about the humans in it, not just selling products and making money," said Brønn. She's hopeful these marketing efforts are an indication that brands are sincere in their desire to be better global citizens.[26]

A NEW ERA IN MARKETING

Welcome to the age of the "Conscious Consumer."

As the Gillette campaign shows us, to build a successful brand in 2019, you must take a stand. During the last ten years, large swaths of consumers have begun to demand that companies take a stand on social, political, and environmental issues. The brands that are the most clear and genuine about what their values are will be the brands that win going forward.

The president decides to place a ban on entry to the country on several majority-Muslim countries? Your company's CEO is expected to publicly support or condemn the policy.

A certain state in the United States decides to create legislation on where individuals of a certain sexual orientation can

---

26 Ibid.

or cannot go to the restroom? What does your company's leadership have to say about that?

Seventeen high school students are gunned down in Parkland, Florida, and the gunman used a firearm that is readily available at your sporting goods store? How will your sporting goods store respond? Will you continue to sell that weapon?

Today's consumer in the United States, and across the world, cares about what your brand cares about. There is no escaping it. Your company or organization must define: What you stand for, Whom you stand for, and Why you stand for it.

If you say you stand for one thing, and your leadership or employees' actions contradict what you said, your brand may never recover from the public relations fury that today's media and consumers will unleash on you.

**

When you look at some of the consumer research done over the last ten years, a funny thing happens. You see that consumers are overwhelmingly demanding that businesses deliver value beyond the bottom line, and you see that business executives understand that their business must both "do well and do good." However, businesses have yet to make the full shift to purpose-driven business practices. Let's take a look at the data.

The 2018 Deloitte Millennial Survey reached over ten thousand millennials from thirty-six countries. About forty percent of those polled believe the goal of business should be to "improve society."[27] According to Antonia Zappulla, CEO designate of the Thomson Reuters Foundation, by 2020, millennials will make up forty percent of all consumers, influencing about $40 billion in annual sales.[28]

A 2014 Nielsen report showed that fifty-five percent of consumers are willing to pay extra for products and services from companies committed to having a positive social and environmental impact.[29]

Sounds like big business, doesn't it? Not only does the largest generation in human history believe that businesses should improve society, but also many consumers across all age

27 Deloitte Touche Tohmatsu Limited. "Millennials disappointed in business, unprepared for Industry 4.0." 2018 Deloitte Millennial Survey. (Accessed October 4, 2019)

28 Zappulla, Antonio. "The Future Of Business? Purpose, Not Just Profit." *World Economic Forum.* Jan. 17th, 2019. (Accessed September 30, 2019.)

29 "Consumer-Goods' Brands That Demonstrate Commitment To Sustainability Outperform Those That Don't". 2015. *Nielsen.Com.* (Accessed September 30, 2019).

groups are already willing to pay more for a product that aligns with their social and environmental values!

How are the big wigs at most companies responding to this data? Well, it appears they understand the growing trend of conscious consumerism, but are they realigning their business strategy to match the demands of the 2019 customer?

According to *The Business Case for Purpose*, a 2014 EY/Harvard Business Review Analytic Services global research study,

- Eighty-seven percent of business executives believe companies perform best over time if their purpose goes beyond profit.
- Eighty-nine percent say that purpose-driven organizations encourage greater employee satisfaction, eighty-five percent better customer advocacy, and eighty-one percent higher-quality products and services
- Eighty percent of business executives state that business purpose increases customer loyalty
- Despite nearly ninety percent of executives saying they understand the importance of benefiting local and global society, only forty-six percent of them say their purpose informs operational or strategic decision making.[30]

---

30 Keller, Valerie. "The Business Case for Purpose" 2014. *Hbr.Org.* (Accessed September 30 2019.)

What is the C-suite missing here? Business leaders seem to understand the importance of doing well and doing good, but they do not seem to feel enough pressure—yet—to fully shift their business models and their brand promises. This missing piece will spell trouble for their organizations.

As Anne Bahr Thompson writes in *Do Good: Embracing Brand Citizenship to Fuel Both Purpose and Profit*, "Ultimately, people are demanding greater value for their dollar than ever before, and businesses must holistically align brand development with sustainability and corporate citizenship initiatives."[31]

What implications does this understanding of the new mandate for brand development and business strategy aligning with purpose have for the sponsorship marketing world?

**

Neill Duffy is an advocate for purpose as the preferred business philosophy of the twenty-first century and the founder of Purpose + Sport, an agency dedicated to inspiring the business of sport to do good and do well. Neill has spent the majority of his career in the sports industry at Octagon, a leading worldwide sports agency at which he served as

---

31 Bahr Thompson, Anne. *Do Good: Embracing Brand Citizenship to Fuel Both Purpose and Profit*. HarperCollins, 2017.

group managing director of South Africa, and president of Europe Middle East Africa.

When I interviewed him, Neill gave a dire warning to sports industry professionals who ignore this wave of conscious consumers.

"Sports has become fat and lazy, and I think they're going to get their asses kicked if they don't wake up," Duffy told me. "The sponsors are lazy. The agencies are lazy. The teams are lazy."

Duffy went on to tell me that he believes they are not fully prioritizing purpose in their marketing and business practices because the industry has been making money hand over fist for years doing business "the old-fashioned way." Why should a major corporate sponsor, a sports property, or a sports marketing agency such as Neill's old employer, Octagon, change its business model when business is thriving?

Don't get too comfortable if you sit in one of the decision-making seats in the sports industry, Duffy says. Change is coming; in fact, it is already here.

"Young people are becoming more and more disenchanted with traditional professional sports. Just look at eSports: there are now over 500 million followers of eSports, the majority of whom are under twenty-five. Those people are not following the NFL, MLB, or other pro sports that I grew up watching."

As we've outlined earlier in the chapter, those same young people who are watching eSports and following top gamers on Twitch, YouTube, and other platforms, are the same customers who believe that business should be used as a force for good.

I am not claiming that the National Football League, Major League Baseball, or National Basketball Association is at risk of taking a nose-dive in value, any time soon. But each of these leagues, and the owners of the teams in these leagues, expect their businesses to grow year over year, every year. Oh, by the way, the corporate sponsors, whose marketing dollars fuel a large part of that growth, expect their dollars to help them acquire and build relationships with customers over a long period of time.

We are already starting to see a massive influx of sponsorship dollars in eSports. Fortune 500 brands such as AT&T and State Farm are already major sponsors of eSports properties ESL North America, the Overwatch League, and League of Legends. This sponsorship will only continue to grow. What then will the behemoth legacy pro sports leagues do if all of a sudden they lose a generation of consumers to competitive gaming leagues?

It has become clear that most consumers, especially consumers that are under thirty-five years old, demand that the brands they support and buy from must have values that align with theirs. The same principle applies to sports, entertainment, music, and all of the sponsors who associate their brands with these industries.

To appeal to the conscious consumer, sponsorship marketers need to consider both purpose and profit. You should always be thinking about whether you are communicating how your values align with today's consumer values. You should consistently look for ways to integrate social or environmental impact into your campaigns and activations.

**

Writing for the World Economic Forum, Antonia Zappulla claims, "Profit with purpose is set to become the new norm. Up to this point, social enterprise and impact investment have been driving this concept, which has somehow remained confined to a niche. Not anymore. Now, it's all set to change: the CEOs of the future will want their companies to be recognized as forces for good."[32]

---

32 Zappulla, Antonio. "The Future Of Business? Purpose, Not Just Profit." *World Economic Forum.* Jan. 17th, 2019. (Accessed September 30, 2019.)

The sports and entertainment industries cannot take their massive success for granted. But even beyond the business opportunity that purpose-driven marketing presents, what about the impact opportunity?

We know how much athletes and the teams and leagues they play for can influence popular culture. Think about how much of an impact the billions of sponsorship dollars could have on people in need and a planet ailing from human abuse.

Today, leadership in the sports world has an opportunity to make doing good and doing well a priority throughout their business operations.

As we'll explore throughout the rest of this book, there are a number of leading athletes, companies, and teams who have already provided a template for purpose-driven marketing. It is good for business, and it is even better for our world. Let's dive in and look at how they are doing it.

THREE WINS FROM CHAPTER 3

- Conscious Consumerism is the new paradigm in consumer behavior that all companies must be in tune with. The data shows that most consumers, and young consumers in particular, care about the social values of the companies that they buy products from.

- Sports and entertainment marketers are beginning to pick up on the importance of the conscious consumer, although some leaders in the industry, like Neill Duffy, caution that they are not picking up on this fast enough.
- "Profit with purpose is set to become the new norm." It behooves sports and entertainment marketers to shift their marketing strategies right away to adjust to this new reality. There are great examples of legacy brands like Gillette that are already shifting to purpose-driven marketing. Sponsorship is a tremendous tool for brands to tell their authentic impact story, and the principles in this book will help marketers do so effectively.

PART 2

THE FIVE PRINCIPLES OF EFFECTIVE THREE-WIN SPONSORSHIP

CHAPTER 4

BEGIN WITH THE THIRD WIN IN MIND

———

"We started with a vision that spoke right to the heart of the 50th anniversary: we didn't want to just bring the Super Bowl to our region, we aspired to do it in a way that would set a new standard. Just as the NFL wanted to celebrate their past, we also knew this was an opportunity for them to celebrate the Big Game and make a statement about its future."

—PAT GALLAGHER AND STEPHANIE MARTIN

**

Begin with the end in mind is habit number two on author Stephen Covey's list of the *7 Habits of Highly Successful People,* a book first published in 1989.

As Covey describes in his best-selling business book, this habit is about imagination. It is about "the ability to envision in your mind what you cannot at present see with your eyes. It is based on the principle that all things are created twice. There is a mental (first) creation, and a physical (second) creation."[33]

Pro athletes talk all the time about beginning their seasons in spring training or training camp with *one goal in mind*: to win the league championship. It is the unifying vision that brings a team together and inspires players to work harder than they've ever worked before. That vision becomes the rallying cry for the team and spurs its members to perform to the best of their abilities during the season.

Taking a page out of the pro athlete's playbook is often a good idea in the business world, and having intentionality and purpose to your work can similarly improve performance and outcomes for your business.

---

33 Covey, Stephen. *The 7 Habits of Highly Effective People: Powerful Lessons in Personal Change.* Simon & Schuster, 2013.

Successful Three-Win sponsorships are no different. When sponsors and sponsorship seekers come together to plan out a deal, they have to align on the core objectives of the sponsorship. As we outlined in Part 1 of this book, successful sponsorships in the twenty-first century need to deliver value to the target markets and align with their core social, political, and environmental beliefs.

The first principle of Three-Win sponsorships is *intention*. It is critical to begin sponsorship deals with the intention of creating social and environmental impact for the target audience. Without the initial vision and mission centered around purpose and causes near and dear to your target market's heart, your sponsorship deals will not reach their full potential to connect meaningfully with customers and fans.

To demonstrate this principle in action, let's take a look at how the organizers of one of the largest sporting events in the world achieved tremendous amounts of success by leading with a clear intention of social good.

SUPER BOWL 50 LEADS WITH PURPOSE

Every February, the biggest spectacle in US sports descends upon a single American city and dominates the headlines—and that city—for two weeks straight. The Super Bowl has become the most iconic event in US sports, but one Super

Bowl stands out from the rest when it comes to almost every key success metric: Super Bowl 50 at Levi's Stadium in the San Francisco Bay Area.

When the final accounting was completed by the Host Committee, Super Bowl 50 had become the most shared, most participatory, and most giving Super Bowl ever, all delivered in a "net positive" way—socially, environmentally and economically.

The accolades for Super Bowl 50 could go on and on. But how did the Super Bowl 50 Host Committee, the San Francisco 49ers, and the Bay Area pull this off?

In their book, *Big Game, Bigger Impact*, Pat Gallagher and Stephanie Martin describe in great detail how the Host Committee set an ambitious goal of "redefining the Super Bowl experience." Gallagher served as the executive vice president of marketing, partnerships and communication for the Host Committee, while Martin played the role of vice president of marketing and communications.

From the beginning, as they set out to find Bay Area companies to seed the Bid Committee's operations, Gallagher and Bid Committee Chairman Daniel Lurie put purpose first. Gallagher estimated that the San Francisco Super Bowl 50 bid would need to raise at least $30 million in commitments from companies who would support its efforts to bring the Super Bowl to the region.

At the time, Lurie ran Tipping Point, a charitable organization built to eradicate poverty in San Francisco. During a meeting at the Tipping Point office, Gallagher put the number "25%" on a white board. This number was meant to signify that the Host Committee would "devote a quarter out of every dollar [they] raised from corporate partnerships to go to nonprofits in our region," Gallagher recalled. "We all wanted to be involved in something that had the potential to deliver real impact. It felt bold, but it also felt right."[34]

Lurie and Gallagher's mind-set was "With the region's leadership in philanthropy, we believed a significant community investment might make this project really resonate with local leaders."[35]

Born out of that meeting was the vision for the fiftieth anniversary of the Super Bowl. As Gallagher wrote, "We started with a vision that spoke right to the heart of the 50th anniversary: we didn't want to just bring the Super Bowl to our region, we aspired to do it in a way that would set a new

---

34 Martin, Stephanie and Pat Gallagher. *Big Game Bigger Impact: How the Bay Area Redefined the Super Bowl Experience and the Lessons That Can Apply to Any Business.* Motivational Press, 2017.
35 Ibid.

standard. Just as the NFL wanted to celebrate their past, we also knew this was an opportunity for them to celebrate the Big Game and make a statement about its future."[36]

"Redefining the Super Bowl" became the core mantra for Gallagher, Lurie and the entire Host Committee. They believed that their true differentiator was their legacy initiative.

Host Committee CEO Keith Bruce and Pat Gallagher took this purpose-driven pitch to the most influential companies in Silicon Valley in search of enough funding to show the NFL that they were serious about hosting Super Bowl 50.

Keith Bruce had been recruited to lead the Host Committee after a long career as president of SportsMark, during which he worked on many Olympics, World Cups, and Super Bowls. He had the necessary experience executing the largest sporting events in the world to lead the San Francisco Bay Area Super Bowl 50 Host Committee.

In early 2013, Bruce and Gallagher knew that the first big corporate sponsors that they landed would make a big difference in their success at landing subsequent partners.

---

36   Ibid.

Gallagher was connected with Google CBO Nikesh Arora, and over a fifteen-minute phone call he received a minimum $2 million pledge from Google, influenced greatly by the vision of making an impact on the Bay Area community.

Soon after, Apple CEO Tim Cook got in touch with Gallagher's team, indicating that Apple was in as well. Apple wanted to pledge a minimum of $2 million and provide in-kind Apple products to help the Host Committee team run its business operations.

Gallagher recalls in "Big Game" being somewhat stunned that two of the largest companies in the world were so easily convinced to commit serious dollars to their efforts. Why did Apple and Google say yes so quickly? He reflected, "What immediately connected with the leadership at both Google and Apple was how this event had the real possibility of leaving a legacy for generations to come. The concept of directing 25% of their partnership funds to benefit the community made the opportunity feel more concrete."[37]

With two big dominoes down in Apple and Google, the Super Bowl 50 Host Committee was able to attract some of the leading companies in Silicon Valley and the greater Bay Area to pledge almost $30 million. Its impressive list of sponsors

---

37   Ibid.

included Boston Consulting Group, Dignity Health, Gap Inc., Hewlett-Packard, Intel, San Francisco Travel, Seagate, ValueAct Capital, and Yahoo.

Storytelling played a huge part in the success of Gallagher's sponsorship efforts. He wrote that "what made the difference was weaving purpose into every part of the presentation and enabling our stakeholders to envision the pride they would feel when it was all said and done. Simply put, we emphasized what all this work was really about: the people in our community and not just football."[38]

A "NET POSITIVE" APPROACH TO THE BIG GAME

Neill Duffy, whom we met in Chapter 3, was named the chair of the Sustainability Committee for Super Bowl 50 in 2012.

Normally, an event as large as the Super Bowl can be a breeding ground for all kinds of waste and excess. From food waste to carbon emissions to overall human waste created, it's not unusual for Super Bowls to create a negative environmental impact for the host city. At the same time, Super Bowls are capable of creating massive amounts of economic impact for the host city.

---

38 Ibid.

Duffy and the Host Committee leadership determined from the very beginning that they would put on the Super Bowl with a "net positive" approach. Meaning that they would "[leverage] Super Bowl 50 as a platform to do good for the entire Bay Area-socially, environmentally and economically."

From an environmental sustainability standpoint, that meant they would operate major activations and experiential marketing components to the event with clean energy and that recycling would be encouraged. Super Bowl City, which was a massive fan village in the heart of San Francisco, was operated with Pacific Gas and Electric Company clean energy— ninety-one percent of temporary power was supplied by Neste renewable diesel generators and two percent of power from hydrogen fuel cell generators.

Food waste and sustainable product use was also considered, as 860 pounds of Super Bowl City food was recovered and donated to local food banks through Food Runners. 162,000 compostable cups, 10,000 bamboo boats and plates, 9,000 eco-friendly cups, 5,000 eco-friendly disposable plates, and 3,000 wine glasses were used throughout the fan village.

The "net positive" intention guided Duffy and the Host Committee's actions, and enabled them to pull off "the greenest Super Bowl ever," and set the standard for all major sporting events with regard to reduction of carbon emissions, food waste, and use of single-use plastics. Super Bowl 50 showed the sports industry that it is entirely possible to run massive sporting events without harming the environment.

**

It may be easy to structure sponsorships the old-fashioned way, but is it effective? Super Bowl 50 and the leaders on the Host Committee who helped pull it off proved that by beginning with the Third Win in mind, they could attract some of the largest, most influential companies in the world to sponsor their event. However, they did not attract Google, Apple, and other Fortune 500 companies by promising the world and failing to deliver.

Super Bowl 50's organizers fulfilled their vision to pull off the big game in a "net positive" way and left a legacy of social impact in the Bay Area that should benefit its residents for years to come. They also exceeded expectations in the number of Bay Area residents who attended a Super Bowl event, the number of times their content was shared on social media, and the amount of media exposure the event received. In other words, they met or exceeded all of their key business objectives because of their purpose-driven intention, not in spite of it.

Brands and properties can learn from leaders like Pat Gallagher, Stephanie Martin, and Neill Duffy and begin applying this principle to their sponsorships right away. Intention drives better business results and better outcomes for the community.

Stephen Covey never said in *7 Habits* that building the habits of an effective person would be easy, nor am I saying that building the habit of "beginning with the Third Win in mind" will be easy. However, I am suggesting that if you want to build effective sponsorships in the twenty-first century, you will want to build the habit of *intention* to do good for your target markets into the core of your deals.

THREE WINS FROM CHAPTER 4

- The first principle of effective Three-Win Sponsorship is **"Begin with the Third Win in mind."** This principle is about being **intentional** from the very beginning of a partnership between sponsor and sponsorship seeker so that each party puts purpose and social impact at the heart of their deal.
- Super Bowl 50 in the San Francisco Bay Area provides a template for any sponsorship seeker on how and why to follow the first principle. Pat Gallagher, Stephanie Martin, and the entire Host Committee put purpose at the core of the event's mission by devoting twenty-five

percent of sponsorship funds raised to charitable initiatives benefiting the Bay Area and its residents. Large companies like Google, Apple, and Intel signed seven-figure deals **because** of that opportunity, not in spite of it.

- It will require a shift in mindset for both sponsorship seekers and sponsors to build Three-Win sponsorships the right way. Both parties should come to the table with a vision of the good they want to do for the target market and define a shared purpose from the outset of their partnership.

CHAPTER 5

GOT TO BE TRUE TO MYSELF

——

"Authenticity is about being true to who you are, even when everyone else wants you to be someone else."

—MICHAEL JORDAN

**

Authenticity has become a buzzword.

The word gets tossed around so frequently at marketing and sponsorship-related conferences and forums that, unfortunately, it seems to have lost some of its meaning. What does it actually mean for a brand to be "authentic" in its marketing and communications with consumers? Why have marketers become so obsessed with being "authentic"?

Personally, I blame Google, Facebook, and Twitter for this new obsession for brand marketers. Let me explain.

When consumers made buying decisions in years past—pre-Internet—the first place they would likely turn to evaluate a product or service was their friends or family members. Consider a consumer living in the early 1990s named Bridget.

Bridget is trying to decide which new car or van she should buy for her family. Bridget asks her friend Jonathan how he likes his Chrysler Town & Country minivan, and Jonathan either says he loves the car or hates the car, and Bridget uses that information to make a purchasing decision herself.

Brands also try to influence Bridget's buying decision through purchase of advertisements in other places where they might be able to capture her attention—on television, on the radio, in magazines, or in the newspaper. Unfortunately for the brands trying to influence Bridget, no matter how many touch points they had with her through their marketing campaigns, it was very difficult for them to measure why she decided to buy the Chrysler minivan. On the flip side, brands in the '90s didn't have to worry as much about

Bridget's frustration with her Town & Country. If her van broke down a ton and she wanted to bad mouth Chrysler's brand, she could only air her grievances to her immediate friends and family. Her influence on consumer buying behavior was limited.

Now let's consider a consumer named Marcus, who's looking to buy a new couch for his apartment in the year 2019. Marcus may first get the idea to look for a new couch after he was served an ad on his Instagram feed for a new Wayfair couch that was fifteen percent off. He may flip through the photos of their couches there on Instagram and view the comments under the ad to see what other people—whom he's never met before in his life—are saying about Wayfair's couches. But Marcus doesn't buy just yet.

About five days later, Marcus has some free time and decides to look up the Google reviews for Wayfair couches. He sees an average of only 3.8 stars for the couch he originally saw on Instagram, and one customer's comment that "this couch looks great but stains soooo easily" really turns him off from Wayfair. The final straw comes once Marcus goes onto his Twitter account and searches for "Wayfair couches" to see what the masses have to say about them. It only takes about thirty-five seconds of scrolling through a feed of negative tweets before Marcus realizes that he should take his search for a new couch someplace else.

(By the way, this situation is completely hypothetical, and I'm sure Wayfair has wonderful couches.)

The point is, because of the tools and the networks available on the internet, consumers have never been more powerful. They have the ability, at any time, to leave a review about your product on Amazon or Google, or to write a searing Tweet about why your brand is so terrible.

It must be terrifying to be in charge of a brand's reputation in today's consumer environment—every product you put out, every marketing campaign you run, can be scrutinized publicly on the Internet for every future customer to see.

Whereas Bridget could only impact her immediate network of friends and family members during the early '90s, Marcus can pick up his iPhone and send a Tweet to his 550 followers—and the hundreds of millions of other Twitter users to see—that slams a company for its poor customer service or inadequate product. Consumers have acquired a great deal of power and influence over fellow consumers.

In my opinion, this newly empowered consumer is why authenticity is so important. Consumers in 2019 can and will call out your brand if they sniff a hint of inauthentic messaging or marketing. They can see through the BS, and they can put you on blast at any moment if they feel like it.

The power of consumers is a reality that all marketers must keep in mind, and it is especially important for sponsorship marketers to understand.

＊＊

The second principle of Three-Win sponsorships is **authenticity**. Buzzword or not, the very best sponsorship professionals understand that their deals must be activated in a way that is genuine to the brand's story, the property's story, and the target market's story. When thinking about sponsorships built for social good, it is even more critical to structure your sponsorships in an authentic way. If you don't, consumers will bury your brand on Twitter.

To understand the principle of authenticity better, let's look at how one of the most iconic sports brands of all time stayed true to itself in the face of a polarizing athlete endorsement campaign.

THE 30TH ANNIVERSARY "JUST DO IT" CAMPAIGN

On Monday, September 3, 2018, former San Francisco 49ers quarterback Colin Kaepernick posted a photo on his personal Instagram page. The close-up, black and white photo of Kaepernick's face had two lines of white text superimposed over his nose, which read, "Believe in something. Even if it means sacrificing everything." At the bottom of the photo was the iconic "swoosh" logo of Nike, along with their equally iconic tagline, "Just do it."

Kaepernick's post was the launch of an advertising campaign designed to celebrate the thirtieth anniversary of Nike's "Just Do It" brand motto. The campaign, and Kaepernick's inclusion as a lead endorser, quickly turned into an international news story and political firestorm in the United States.

As Jill Avery and Koen Pauwels cover in their Harvard Business School case study titled "Brand Activism: Nike and Colin Kaepernick," the choice of Colin Kaepernick as the face of Nike's latest "Just Do It" campaign sparked a great deal emotions, both positive and negative, among consumers.[39]

At this time, Kaepernick's public reputation had been tied to his protest of police brutality, racism, and social injustice. In 2016, during his tenure with the 49ers, Kaepernick began silently protesting by kneeling during the playing of the National Anthem before games. It is customary in American culture to stand during the National Anthem, and Kaepernick's protest was perceived by some citizens as disrespectful

---

39 Avery, Jill, and Koen Pauwels. "Brand Activism: Nike and Colin Kaepernick." Harvard Business School Case 519-046, December 2018. (Revised September 2019.)

toward the country and the men and women who have served in the US military.

In truth, the anthem protest was intended to bring attention to the larger Black Lives Matter movement that had been spreading across the country. "I am not going to show pride in a flag for a country that oppresses black people and people of color," Kaepernick said of his demonstration.[40]

Avery and Pauwels describe in their case study how, "Kaepernick's protest proved to be highly polarizing along racial, generational, and political lines." A poll during the 2016 season named him the most disliked player in the league, with thirty-seven percent of Caucasians saying they "disliked him a lot" and forty-two percent of African Americans saying they "liked him a lot." Forty-six percent of Nike's recent customers, however, viewed him favorably, while twenty-three percent of recent customers viewed him unfavorably. Similarly, Kaepernick was viewed far more favorably by Democrats than Republicans, and by younger citizens than older citizens.

Kaepernick became an NFL free agent after the end of the 2016 season but went through the entire 2017 offseason

---

40   Petrarca, Emilia. "What Nike's 'Just Do It' Slogan Means with Colin Kaepernick behind it," *The Cut*, September 5, 2018, (Accessed October 7, 2019).

without receiving a single job offer from an NFL team. In fall 2017, Kaepernick accused NFL owners of "blackballing" him, or conspiring together to not hire him in order to avoid the political baggage associated with his personal brand.[41]

Around the same time, Nike executives were considering whether the company wanted to cancel the endorsement deal with the former star quarterback, which he had signed in 2011 after being drafted in the second round of the NFL draft by the San Francisco 49ers. When, in 2018, rival athletic footwear and apparel brand Adidas expressed interest in signing Kaepernick to an endorsement deal, the pressure was on Nike to decide how it wanted to move forward with the relationship.

Kaepernick's legal case against the NFL and its owners found sufficient evidence of collusion to support going to trial. GQ magazine named him its Citizen of the Year and Amnesty International awarded him its Ambassador of Conscience award.

Nike decided to stick with the polarizing Kaepernick and elevate his status among its roster of athlete endorsers. So when it released the thirtieth-anniversary "Just Do It" campaign,

---

41   Avery, Jill, and Koen Pauwels. "Brand Activism: Nike and Colin Kaepernick." Harvard Business School Case 519-046, December 2018. (Revised September 2019.)

Nike's brand leadership team members were taking a calculated risk. It knew full well how Kaepernick's high profile protest might rub some of its consumer base the wrong way, yet they moved forward with it anyway.

Social media platforms went completely insane after the September 2018 Instagram post on Kaepernick's page. A large number of Nike supporters chimed in with words of praise and encouragement for Nike and Kaepernick's partnership. However, a great deal of social media accounts began posting photos and videos of their #BoycottNike stance, with some customers even cutting Nike logos off of their socks or burning Nike footwear or apparel they already owned.

The critical and positive reviews from business and political pundits began pouring in on both sides of the campaign, with President Donald Trump even chiming in with his own negative review on Twitter. One thing was clear, though: Nike's stand with Colin Kaepernick had captured a ton of attention.

Some campaign reviewers asked: how could Nike be so "arrogant" and take such a massive risk at "alienating" so many of their potential consumers?

Others were much more complimentary, such as Tim Crow, CEO of sports marketing firm Synergy, who wrote, "Like all smart companies, Nike realizes that what it makes is not what it is about. It needs to stand for something within culture. In this instance, it's on the side of athletes, young black kids, civil rights proponents and people who are against Donald Trump."[42]

But is brand activism new for Nike? Let's look back at Nike's track record of brand activism to see how genuine this 2018 campaign was for the company. Its history indicates that its support of Colin Kaepernick and his cause should have come as no surprise.

NIKE'S TRACK RECORD OF BRAND ACTIVISM

A sports industry insider, discussing the thirtieth-anniversary "Just Do It" campaign, told The New York Times in 2018, "Nike from Day 1 has really been a brand that has stood up to and stood for things that were important to them and important to their athletes, so I think there is a little precedence there."

Harvard Business School's case study cites a pretty impressive resume of brand activism by the company: "Nike was the first brand to feature a HIV positive athlete in the midst of

---

42 Friend, Nick. "Just do it, Kaepernick and the NFL: Why Nike doesn't care about burning trainers," *SportsProLive*, September 6, 2018. (Accessed 10/7/2019).

the AIDS crisis, the first brand to feature an amputee athlete, and the first brand to feature a LGBT athlete."

The company had also taken stands in support of Title IX, the federal civil rights law that disallowed discrimination based on gender in education programs that received federal assistance, and on behalf of African American athletes and Muslim athletes.

It's worth mentioning, too, that Nike's manufacturing processes were heavily scrutinized during the 1990s for being unethical and inhumane in its treatment of workers in Southeast Asian countries where they housed their factories. The company took steps to open up its supply chain and factories to third-party investigators, who could insure they were operating them in a just, humane way.

BUSINESS OUTCOMES OF THE THIRTIETH-ANNIVERSARY CAMPAIGN

So how did Nike's sponsorship of Colin Kaepernick affect their business? Did it do irreparable damage to their business, or did it make their connection even deeper with its key customers? The numbers tell the story in pretty clear terms.

After the campaign launch on Colin Kaepernick's personal Instagram, Nike plastered the ad on billboards in New York

City and San Francisco, then built on the campaign by releasing a two-minute video advertisement titled "Dream Crazy." Narrated by Kaepernick, the ad featured fellow Nike endorsers Serena Williams and LeBron James, along with low-profile but inspiring athletes overcoming personal challenges to compete. With an aspirational message, Kaepernick himself appeared at the end of the video saying "So don't ask if your dreams are crazy; ask if they're crazy enough."

In a company press release that accompanied the video debut, Nike wrote, "For 30 years, the 'Just Do It' mantra has been a motivational call for athletes nationwide, across all sports, and all levels of play. To celebrate that rich diversity... "Dream Crazy" focuses on a collection of stories that represent athletes who are household names and those who should be. The common denominator: All leverage the power of sport to move the world forward."[43]

"Dream Crazy" first received airtime on Wednesday, September 5, 2018—the day before the first game of the NFL season. Nike proceeded to air it during the opening game and throughout the entire first weekend of NFL games.

Nike CEO Mark Parker announced at the company's annual meeting in September 2018 that the company cre-

---

43 Nike, Inc. (2018) "A Crazy Dream Becomes Reality When You Just Do It," *Nike.com*, (Accessed October 7, 2019)

ated a Kaepernick shoe and T-shirt and would be donating a portion of the proceeds from their sales to Kaepernick's Know Your Rights Camp, a nonprofit dedicated to self-empowerment, raising awareness about opportunities in higher education, and instruction about safely interacting with law enforcement.

Concerning the campaign and Kaepernick's role in it, Parker stated, "Colin is one of the most inspirational athletes of our time, as well as the other athletes featured in the spot. Together, I think they're a good example of leveraging the power of sport to help move the world forward. We are very proud to be a part of that."

How did the market respond to the bold political and social statement by Nike embedded in its thirtieth-anniversary "Just Do It" campaign?

From an earned media perspective, the company seemed to have an overall positive result. "Just Do It" received 400,000 mentions on social media platforms on September 4 alone. Within one hour of its release, the "Dream Crazy" ad had more than five million views on YouTube. A month later, it had more than eighty million views on Twitter, Instagram, and YouTube. On Instagram, Nike added roughly 170,000 followers in the aftermath of the campaign.

Apex Marketing reported that Nike received $163.5 million in earned media value in the first three days alone.[44]

Consumer sentiment was a mixed bag. A Twitter poll with more than 35,000 people suggested that one in five people had a negative reaction to the campaign. Of those polled, twenty-nine percent said they were more likely to buy Nike products, twenty-one percent said they were less likely to buy Nike products after viewing the campaign, and fifty percent said it would not affect their buying decision.

According to CNN, forty-four percent of those ages eighteen to thirty-four supported Nike's decision to use Kaepernick, while fifty-two percent of those ages thirty-five to forty-four supported the decision.

It should be noted that not every metric around consumer sentiment was positive in Nike's favor. Morning Consult reported that Nike's favorability rating dropped by double digits; from a net plus-69 to a net plus-35 favorable impression among consumers. "As the negative buzz set in, consumer sentiment followed, with favorability and purchasing consideration dropping," claimed a Morning Consult analyst.

44 Robinson, Charles (2018) "Colin Kaepernick's commercial is a big hit with consumers, according to industry group," *Yahoo Sports*, September 6, 2018. (Accessed 10/7/2019)

With that said, Nike's campaign dominated conversations online and offline. "Overall, Nike increased its share of positive conversations in the athletic apparel category, thus crowding out discussions about other competitors," wrote Avery and Pauwels.

Breaking down the performance of the "Dream Crazy" ad, Nike achieved remarkable awareness results. "In September and October of 2018, 50% of all U.S. consumers aged 18+ reported seeing an advertisement for Nike in the past two weeks. This marked the brand's highest advertising awareness score since *YouGov* began tracking the metric in late 2012," according to Ted Marzilli of YouGov.

Another advertising analyst, Ace Metrix, "found the ad scored high marks with a broad base of the consumer population. 'Dream Crazy' saw strong resonance among [Generation Z] and Millennial audiences [on average, Ace Scores were 33% above the norm]. Older viewers, those among [Generation] X, positively regarded the ad as well, but to a lesser degree than those younger than them."

Plus, when Ace Metrix polled consumers on how it would impact their plans to spend money with Nike, thirteen percent said less likely to purchase—ten percent of Millennials and six percent of Generation Z—while fifty-six percent said more likely to purchase."

How did the "Just Do It" campaign affect Nike's bottom line? "Nike's online sales reportedly grew 31% from the Sunday of Labor Day weekend through the following Tuesday, as compared with a 17% gain recorded for the same period in 2017," according to Edison Trends.[45]

In addition, Thomson Reuters Proprietary Research noted that "Nike sold out far more items online between September 3 and September 13 than in the 10-day period before the ad came out."[46]

On Wall Street, Nike's stock took an initial dip by about three percent while Adidas dropped 2.4% and Puma dropped two percent. In the weeks following the release of "Dream Crazy" however, Nike stock increased back in line with its overall positive trend for the year.

Between Tuesday, September 4, and Friday, September 28, Nike's share price and market capitalization grew from $79.60 to $84.72 per share and $127.4 billion and $135.6 billion, respectively.[47]

---

45 Linnane, Ciara (2018) "Nike's online sales jumped 31% after Kaepernick campaign, data show," *MarketWatch*, September 17, 2018 (Accessed October 7, 2019).

46 Reuters (2018), "Nike's Kaepernick ad spurs spike in sold out items," *Business of Fashion*, September 19, 2018 (Accessed October 7, 2019).

47 Nasdaq (2018) "Nike, Inc. Common Stock (NKE) Quote Summary and Data," *Nasdaq*, (Accessed October 7, 2019).

Parker told Wall Street analysts on the company's quarterly earnings call that the campaign had yielded "record engagement with the brand," proclaiming, "We feel very good and are very proud of the work we've been doing. We know it's resonated quite strongly with consumers."[48]

TAKEAWAYS

Without question, Nike's thirtieth-anniversary "Just Do It" campaign made an impact on its business. By choosing sides in a fiery political debate, Nike took on significant risk of alienating consumers who disagreed with their support of Colin Kaepernick and what he stood for.

The "Just Do It" story provides some great lessons for brand leaders. First and foremost, if your company decides to take a stand on a political or social issue, it must have a long track record of genuinely supporting that side of the issue. Consumers can smell out inauthentic messaging and positioning in your marketing like bloodhounds, so flip-flopping on issues is not tenable if you want your campaign to be well-received.

---

48   Nike, Inc (2018) "Nike, Inc. (NKE) CEO Mark Parker on Q1 2019 Results – Earnings Call Transcript," *Seeking Alpha,* September 25, 2018 (Accessed October 7, 2019).

Second, think long and hard before you join in on deeply political debates, and be prepared for negative backlash along with the positive feelings from your supporters. The US political scene was hyperpolarized in 2018. Nike made the decision to elevate Kaepernick, knowing full well that a large segment of the American population disliked and disagreed with his political views. As Nick Friend of SportsPro Live wrote, "This is a brand that, in the midst of volatile global political climates, [chose] to involve itself. This is a brand that stares at a social issue and jumps over the fence."[49]

From a pure business perspective, this type of risk is not for every brand. So in evaluating whether or not to jump into the political fray, Nike counted on its long-term reputation as a brand that stood with and stood for athletes who "move the world forward." It also realized that while its brand might take a hit with older consumers in the short-term, over the long-term, it felt like it would win over the hearts and minds of younger, more progressive-thinking consumers.

Nike's decision brings us to the final lesson—make bold statements with your brand using a long-term lens on your brand identity. By running the Kaepernick "Believe in something" ad in 2018, Nike made it clear to the marketplace on what

---

49   Friend, Nick. "Just do it, Kaepernick and the NFL: Why Nike doesn't care about burning trainers," *SportsProLive*, September 6, 2018. (Accessed October 7, 2019).

its brand stood for in 2018 and in 2028. It must have studied Kaepernick's favorability ratings among younger adults and known that its business could continue to grow and sustain itself if it could grab hold of the eighteen – to thirty-four-year-old consumer. It was good business for the long term, in Nike's estimation, to take some heat in the short term, if it meant that it would continue to dominate its category for generations to come.

David Klein of Marketing News wrote about the direct correlation between corporate social responsibility and business strategy in a piece in 2018: "Social responsibility only works if it is first and foremost commercially responsible. No brand can actually go as far as Kaepernick says and sacrifice everything, so the Nike campaign has to be assessed for what it really is: a business decision...in a commercial context, purpose is a means to an end."[50]

We may have to wait a few years to fully understand the impact of Nike's thirtieth-anniversary "Just Do It" campaign and continue to watch closely as the brand leverages sponsorship of elite athletes to tell its brand story. But by choosing to support athletes who inspire the world to move forward and embrace diversity, Nike has carved out a unique place in the consumer world.

---

50   Klein, David (2018). "Experts Weigh In: Was Nike's Colin Kaepernick ad a good idea?" *Marketing News,* (Accessed October 7, 2019)

**

Nike exemplified the importance of long-term consistency with respect to delivering authentic athlete endorsements. However, another important thing to consider and understand when building sponsorships is what your target audience values the most. I found this lesson by getting in touch with one of the stewards of US Bank's sponsorship portfolio to learn about how they stay authentic and genuine with their sponsorships by listening and responding to their target audience.

Ania Sponaski is the vice president of global sponsorship consulting at GMR Marketing. A native of Canada, she got her start in the sponsorship marketing industry by working with VANOC, the organizing committee for the 2010 Winter Olympic Games in Vancouver, British Columbia.

Sponaski describes herself as a "geeky" fan of the Olympics, who has always been drawn to the values that the Olympic Games represent. As she worked on the Olympic organizing group for Vancouver 2010, she always tried to think about ways to create more compelling stories for the brand partners coming in to sponsor the Olympics that would tie back into the values extolled by the games.

She joined a leading sponsorship consulting agency, GMR Marketing, in 2011, initially representing Olympic and Paralympic athletes across Europe.

As her career at GMR continued to progress, Sponaski recognized that she had "somehow landed in this position of working with brand clients that were all about purpose."

US BANK REIMAGINES WHAT'S "POSSIBLE"

One such GMR client that is a major practitioner of purpose-driven marketing is US Bank, which is the fifth-largest financial institution in the United States and has grown significantly over the last ten years through acquisitions of several regional banks.

Along with that growth story, US Bank has experienced a bit of an identity crisis at times. At its roots, the company prides itself as a financial institution centered on community banking and genuine connection with its consumers. At the same time, with its scale and technology capabilities, the bank has all of the benefits consumers have come to expect from a major financial institution.

US Bank began working with GMR Marketing in 2016, and Sponaski was assigned as the account lead. At this time, the sponsorship organization did not have a single, unifying framework for their marketing spend.

To begin the revamping of their sponsorship strategy, US Bank's Chief Administrative Officer Kate Quinn challenged GMR to do a full review of companies doing a great job with purpose-driven marketing. Quinn wanted to better understand the type of brands that were already focused in this space and how the bank could best learn from them and follow suit in their efforts.

Sponaski and the GMR team reviewed several companies that seemed to be focusing on community impact through their marketing and brand platforms. A few that stood out were the Always #LikeAGirl program, DICK'S Sporting Goods and its Sports Matter program, and State Farm's sponsorship portfolio in general, which tied into its Neighborhood of Good community engagement platform.

However, Sponaski told me that the takeaway from GMR's research was that "there was still no brand that was leveraging sponsorship to truly tell their brand story from a purpose-driven narrative."

Understanding that her clients at US Bank were eager to stand out from its competition in consumer banking in an authentic way, Sponaski made the recommendation that the bank align its entire sponsorship portfolio with its preexisting community engagement and giving platform, called "Community Possible."

Community Possible was created by US Bank to "close the gap between people and possibility in the areas of Work, Home, and Play," according to its website.[51] The company dedicates its resources and its employees' time to empower small-business owners, help families secure safe and affordable housing, and ensure access to arts, recreation, and play for youth and adults in low – to moderate-income communities.

With a clear vision on how they wanted to communicate with consumers through their sponsorship strategy, GMR and US Bank set out to make an initial investment in their Community Possible platform.

The first major activation came through a stadium naming rights partnership with the Minnesota Vikings. Leveraging the deep connection that Vikings fans have with that team, US Bank made it a priority to connect with these fans through a community health and wellness initiative called Places to Play.

---

51 U.S. Bancorp, 2019. "U.S. Bancorp 2018 Corporate Social Responsibility". *usbank.com*. (Accessed October 7 2019).

Sponaski told me that Places to Play became the first great example of US Bank "showing that they're not going to talk about themselves, they are going to talk about who they are trying to benefit" through sports sponsorship.

Since the launch of Places to Play in 2015, US Bank has invested $1 million to fund play places in Minnesota and grant funding to twenty-five nonprofits dedicated to arts, recreation, and play. In the first three years of partnership with the Vikings, US Bank was able to impact 98,000 people through Places to Play.[52]

COMMUNITY POSSIBLE AND THE CMA

After the success of that partnership, GMR and US Bank went back into the lab to determine their best next investment to build upon Places to Play and the partnership with the Vikings. After a rigorous evaluation process, the team determined that a national sponsorship of the Country Music Association (CMA) would truly connect with its target audience. Sponaski recalled telling the US Bank team: "This is the type of partnership that provides you all of the assets allowing you to tie back into purpose and Community Possible."

---

52   Ibid.

US Bank and the CMA Foundation expanded Places to Play by investing in nonprofits that would provide new musical instruments and music education to students from under-served communities in Cincinnati and Chicago. Through an investment in an organization called Notes for Notes, many Chicago students had an opportunity to go to a studio and record music for free.

"This partnership with the CMA and CMA Foundation supports music education programs that teach important life skills and develop the leaders of tomorrow," said Marsha Cruzan, US Bank Chicago regional president. "Notes for Notes plays a vital part of introducing music to the youth of our communities."[53]

Students taking part in the Harmony Project in Los Angeles were invited to a sound check for the CMA Songwriter Series presented by US Bank in September 2018. Those students were able to meet with Florida Georgia Line stars Brian Kelley and Tyler Hubbard and receive brand-new instruments.

The US Bank and CMA Foundation partnership was so successful because of how authentic the program was for both parties. Tiffany Kerns, executive director of CMA Foundation, said about the partnership, "We are always looking

---

53   Ibid.

for key partners who share our same mission and vision for revitalizing communities and supporting tomorrow's future leaders. The U.S. Bank Places to Play program was able to impact thousands of children in five communities through the power of music — the ultimate unifier and a true catalyst for helping shape our next generation."[54]

Places to Play has been so successful for US Bank in creating a real connection with its target consumers that it doesn't anticipate changing anything, according to Sponaski. If anything, the bank plans to double down on purpose-driven sponsorship. "As US Bank's sponsorship portfolio evolves, community is the first thing we've been focusing on, because we know that is what means the most to their core audience," Sponaski said.

A THREE-WIN MINDSET IN CHARLOTTE

The Charlotte Rail Trail is a 3.5-mile trail that runs through the middle of Charlotte, North Carolina. It connects multiple neighborhoods in the city and has a ton of foot traffic on a daily basis. According to charlotterailtrail.org, "The Rail Trail is *the* place to discover cafés and bars, explore galleries, see artists at work, stumble upon an impromptu concert,

---

54 Ibid.

stroll with your family, or relax on a bench and watch the city come alive around you."[55]

While a walking trail already exists, leaders and developers in the Charlotte community have a vision for turning the Rail Trail into so much more than a walkway. They envision transforming the trail into a hub for social engagement, arts, culture, entertainment, and commerce.

To make this possible, US Bank has stepped up and committed a significant amount of money to complete the transformation of the Charlotte Rail Trail. Sponaski said that it was a perfect tie-in to Community Possible because the bank's investment was "the final piece of the puzzle to come together and build a bridge to connect two parts of the city of Charlotte. US Bank is committing to making that bridge possible."

So what was the motivation for leaders like Kate Quinn and Chris Lee at US Bank to shift their entire sponsorship strategy to align with community engagement? In part, it was because of a minor identity crisis. Sponaski told me they teetered on the fence about what their brand stood for in the marketplace.

---

55 Charlotte Rail Trail (2019) "About — Charlotte Rail Trail". *CharlotteRailTrail*.org. (Accessed October 7, 2019).

At its roots, US Bank is a community-focused bank, but, through a series of big acquisitions, it has become nearly as large as Bank of America, Wells Fargo, and Citi. Leadership asked itself, "How do we balance our community banking roots with our big bank capabilities?"

Ultimately, the bank chose to focus on community banking, but also to communicate that it has all of the technology capabilities that consumers have come to expect from its bank. US Bank found strength in being authentic because they felt it would set them apart from the other big banks. "This was an opportunity for US Bank to break free of the mold and show up as a different kind of bank. They decided to position themselves to consumers by saying, 'We are your community partner,'" said Sponaski.

For Ania Sponaski, the lesson she took away from working with US Bank was something any sponsor or property can apply to their strategy going forward. **"If you don't start putting the consumer at the center of your sponsorship activation, they're not going to choose your business over another; it just won't work."**

＊＊

Nike and US Bank's stories show that authenticity wins with the demanding, powerful twenty-first-century customer.

Because of social media and online review platforms, the stakes are much higher for marketers these days. Sponsors and properties will get better outcomes from their sponsorship deals if they stay true to their genuine brand story and consistent with their messaging over a long period of time.

Most importantly, the authentic and consistent messaging must be in alignment with the customer's values and beliefs. It is not up to the brand to make the customer a part of the brand's story. It is up to the brand to make itself a part of the customer's story.

THREE WINS FROM CHAPTER 5

- The second principle of Three-Win Sponsorship is **authenticity**. Consumers are more powerful than ever, and have tools such as Facebook, Instagram, and Twitter at their disposal to expose your brand if it comes off as disingenuous or fake.
- Nike exemplified the principle of authenticity through its endorsement deal with Colin Kaepernick, and its major thirtieth-anniversary "Just Do It" campaign. The company chose to take a big, bold stand on volatile social and political issues, but it landed well with most consumers because of Nike's long standing track record of supporting athletes' social and political beliefs.

- US Bank discovered that by tying its sports and entertainment sponsorship portfolio to its community engagement platform "Community Possible," it could create stories "that truly mattered to their target audience." Any brand looking to reimagine its sponsorship portfolio should learn from US Bank's emphasis on "putting the consumer at the center of its sponsorship activation."

CHAPTER 6

WASTE NOT, WANT NOT

———

"We cannot choose between growth and sustainability – we must have both."

—PAUL POLMAN, FORMER CEO OF UNILEVER

**

In September 2015, governments from all over the world came together through the platform of the United Nations to develop and agree to a new set of global growth and development goals, which were called the Sustainable Development Goals (SDGs). Then, in December 2015, the Paris Agreement was adopted by 195 countries to combat climate change and adapt to its effects.

The United Nations Sports for Climate Action framework describes the Paris Agreement and SDGs as "two visionary agreements which hold great potential to stabilize our climate, proliferate peace and prosperity, and open opportunity for billions of people."[56]

Unfortunately, potential is different than reality. The Sports for Climate Action framework was created in December 2018 by stakeholders from across the sports industry and UN Climate Change and was originally signed during the UN Climate Change Conference in Katowice, Poland, by the International Olympic Committee (IOC), International Sailing Federation, World Surf League, Forest Green Rovers Football Club, the French Tennis Federation, and the Paris 2024 Summer Olympics.

HSH Prince Albert II of Monaco, chair of the IOC Sustainability and Legacy Commission, spoke during the conference and said of signing the agreement, "With its global reach, universal appeal and the power to inspire and influence millions of people around the globe, sport is uniquely placed to drive global climate action and encourage crowds to join in. As countries here in Katowice prepare to turn their climate

---

56 United Nations Framework Convention for Climate Change (2019) "Sports for Climate Action Framework," Unfcc.Int, (Accessed October 7, 2019)

commitments into reality, we stand ready to leverage the power of sport to support their efforts."[57]

Sports' role in climate change is undeniable, through "associated travel, energy use, construction, catering, and so on." At the same time, the implications of climate change for sport are dire. Among the ten major ways climate change is impacting sport, the Sports for Climate Action framework cites "damage to playing surfaces due to extreme temperatures, extended periods of drought, flooding, and/or pest species extending their natural range," as just a few of the problems sports will have to face as our planet continues to warm.[58]

Because of these existential consequences, the third principle of Three-Win sponsorship is **sustainability**. If leagues, teams, athletes, and brands want to continue to grow and thrive in the twenty-first century, they will need to become part of the solution to Earth's climate crisis.

Fortunately, sport has that incredible platform with which to influence human behavior. In this chapter, we will dive

---

57   UNFCCC, "Sports Launch Climate Action Framework At COP24". 2019. Unfccc.Int. (Accessed October 7, 2019)

58   United Nations Framework Convention for Climate Change (2019) "Sports for Climate Action Framework," Unfcc.Int, (Accessed 10/7/2019)

into how the industry can leverage that platform and activate sustainable behaviors through sponsorship.

SPEARHEADING SUSTAINABILITY IN COLLEGIATE ATHLETICS

If you ask Dave Newport about sustainability in sports and entertainment sponsorship, he will tell you this:

"There is no downside. There is only upside."

Newport is a sustainability professional who has worked in college athletics over the past twenty-plus years. When we spoke for this book, he told me his journey to integrate sustainability into college sports began at the University of Florida in 1999. He was hired to become the sustainability director, reporting directly to the university president. However, it was when he looked at the size of the Florida athletics department, he said to himself, "What an opportunity to change the world."

In 2002, Newport approached the Florida athletic director at the time, Jeremy Foley, and proposed that the football program hold a "zero waste" football game on homecoming. There would be no food waste, no carbon emissions, and no water waste, and Newport promised Foley they would go out and get a corporate sponsor to pay for it. Foley got on board quickly and let Newport run with the idea.

As the homecoming game approached, the Florida athletic department began communicating with its fanbase about the "zero waste" mission for the game. They wanted to both ensure that the Gator fanbase had bought in to the concept and educate them on why it was important. Gator Athletics staff created zero waste signage in parking lots and throughout the football stadium to hammer home the message because it was important for Gator fans to feel like they were a part of the mission.

To get immediate feedback on their sustainable, zero waste homecoming initiative, Newport and his staff went from tailgate to tailgate and from box to box in the stadium to get Gators fans' feedback. The response was overwhelmingly positive. Newport told me that 99.9% of the fans' feedback was positive in support of the zero waste game. He told me that he only received one negative comment that day, from an elderly Gators fan who told him, "Sure, this is great, but why haven't we been doing this all along?"

After the game, when Newport debriefed with Foley, Foley told him, "There's no downside to this." This comment really stuck with Newport and informed the rest of his career.

A NEW LEVEL AT UNIVERSITY OF COLORADO BOULDER

Fast forward to the year 2006. Newport was hired to become the director of the Environmental Center at the University of Colorado, Boulder. CU Boulder's Environmental Center is the largest in the United States and has been operating for over fifty years.

Once he got settled in at the university, it occurred to Newport that he ought to go knocking on the athletic director's door once again. In 2008, that door belonged to Mike Bohn. Lucky for Newport, Bohn was a progressive thinker, much like Jeremy Foley at Florida.

This time, however, Newport was not going to propose a one-off "sustainability day" at the football stadium. Instead, Newport told Bohn, "I'd like to make the entire athletic department sustainable." Newport was surprised when Bohn almost immediately agreed to do so. So he said to Bohn, "Mike, that was awfully easy. How come you said yes so fast?"

"What you don't understand, Dave, is that people don't come here for football on Saturday," Bohn told him. "They come here for community. Sustainability creates community and creates engagement that we can't get in any other way. And oh, by the way, we're going to sell sponsorships against this and save money on our operations."

With the blessing from the athletic director, Newport set out to build the nation's first NCAA Division I sports sustainability program in 2008. They called it Ralphie's Green Stampede.

The results over the last ten to eleven years have been remarkable and have led the University of Colorado, Boulder to become the leading US higher education institution with respect to sustainability. CU has been named the greenest campus by Sierra magazine and became the nation's first Gold-rated campus under the Sustainability Tracking, Assessment and Rating System (STARS).

All of these accolades have been led by the athletics department, starting with Ralphie's Green Stampede. Buffaloes Athletics boasts the greenest unit on campus. Their training and administrative buildings are Leadership in Energy and Environmental Design (LEED) Platinum. Their department is zero waste, zero carbon emissions, zero pesticides, zero net water use, and even features a zero net energy football practice facility.

Newport told me that the purpose of Ralphie's Green Stampede "is to inspire and influence fans to be more sustainable at home, work, and play. It's a purpose built around changing the community and changing people. Every activation we've ever created was to use people's allegiance to the Colorado sports brand as an influencer. Essentially, we tell fans 'If you want to be a good Buff, then you want to act sustainably at home, work, and play.'"

As Mike Bohn told him when he gave him the green light on Ralphie's Green Stampede, "This is all about building community."

"Community means you look like I do, you act like I do, you sing the same songs that I do, and you recycle like I do," Newport said. "So we traffic in creating community around sustainability."

With such a unique positioning as the greenest athletic department in the country, CU, led by Dave Newport, has been able to attract Fortune 500 sponsors including BASF, Pepsi, Wells Fargo, WhiteWave Foods, Eco-Products and Ball Corporation. The reason these companies invested in the Buffs, Newport tells me, is that they wanted to be associated with green consumer behavior. Plus, sponsors realized the need to align with younger consumers values, and sustainability is at or near the top of the list.

Not only that, but the research also shows that brands who are associated with green activation, are held in higher esteem by consumers, and their name is remembered longer and more fondly than those of brands not associated with sustainability programs. Brands gain favor and credibility with consumers by putting their resources behind marketing activations that reinforce environmentally-friendly behavior.

A good example of this principle is the Ralphie's Green Stampede Water for the West program. Water for the West is a pledge that any Colorado Buffaloes fan can take to help conserve Earth's most precious resource—water. Fans can use SMS to text a pledge that they will: 1) Eat less meat 2) Buy less stuff 3) Buy recycled products 4) Recycle at home, work, and play, and 5) Use water and energy efficient appliances.

Citizens in the western United States rely heavily on the Colorado River as their major source for freshwater. "Over 30 million people rely on the Colorado for food, water, recreation, energy, and work. Not to mention the countless species whose survival depends on the river," states the CU athletic department website.[59] Pair this with the fact that the average American uses about two thousand gallons of water a day through the food we eat, energy we use, and the products we buy, and the Colorado River, unfortunately, does not run all the way to the Gulf of Mexico.

To raise awareness, offset CU's water footprint, and counteract the drying up of the Colorado River, the CU Athletic

---

59 University of Colorado Boulder (2016). "Water For The West". UC Boulder Environmental Center. colorado.edu/ecenter (Accessed October 7, 2019).

Department and Ralphie's Green Stampede partnered with Wells Fargo to restore one thousand gallons of water to the river for every pledge made by a Buffs fan. CU tapped its athletes to shoot public service announcement videos for Water for the West, including a Women's Soccer player named Taylor Kornieck, who grew up on the Colorado River in the town of Granby, Colorado. They close these PSAs featuring CU athletes with the call to action, "What kind of Buff will you be?"

SCALING THE GREEN MOVEMENT IN THE PAC-12

Dave Newport has not stopped pursuing his vision to build a more sustainable sports industry at the University of Colorado. In 2015, the rest of the Pac-12 Conference, the NCAA conference that CU has been a part of since 2010, caught wind of Ralphie's Green Stampede and decided that they wanted to be a part of it. So the first step Newport took was to have every Pac-12 athletic department join the Green Sports Alliance, the environmentally focused trade organization that "convenes stakeholders from around the sporting world to promote healthy, sustainable communities where we live and play." The Pac-12 was the first Power 5 NCAA conference with every single school to become a member of the Green Sports Alliance.

From there, Newport convened leaders from every Pac-12 Athletic Department to launch Pac-12 Team Green, "the nation's first college sports sustainability property," in 2018. Pac-12 Team Green was built to "unite all 12 universities for a more sustainable future," and included the creation of the annual Pac-12 Sustainability Conference, the Pac-12 Zero Waste Competition, and the Pac-12 Sustainability Working Group.[60]

Newport and the Pac-12 were then able to convince Unifi, a global textile solutions provider, to become the founding sustainability partner of Pac-12 Team Green. The sponsorship included "grant funding to all 12 of the Conference's member institutions to support sustainability initiatives and increase recycling efforts; work with the Pac-12 and Pac-12 Networks on creating custom content and media assets to feature sustainability programs and support efforts to recycle billions of plastic bottles into fiber; and [serving] as an official sponsor for all Pac-12 championship events."[61]

In building Pac-12 Team Green and helping secure the multifaceted sponsorship with Unifi, Newport proved that *sustainability sells.* In doing so, he has set out to help more sports organizations and corporate partners align on shared sustainability values through sponsorship by building a new

---

60 Pac-12 (2018) "Launch Of "Pac-12 Team Green" Announced". pac-12. com (Accessed October 7, 2019).

61 Pac-12 (2018) "Pac-12 And Unifi Announce Founding Partnership Of Pac-12 Team Green". (Accessed October 7, 2019).

sports marketing and consulting firm called Phase 3 Sports. With the Pac-12 Team Green as their first client, Newport, along with Phase 3 Sports co-founders Monica Rowand and Kevin Dorsey, envisions a day "where every league, every venue, every team, and every corporate partnership have strategic sustainability elements embedded in their purpose and outcomes."

What is holding the industry back from achieving this vision? Newport cites two things: 1) building sponsorships "the old-fashioned way" is still very lucrative, and 2) sports properties have to walk the walk before they talk the talk. "You can't sell a corporate sponsor on your sustainability platform, until you have those sustainability practices built into your business," Newport said.

**

The five principles of the Sports for Climate Action framework[62] are:

1. Undertake systematic efforts to promote greater environmental responsibility.
2. Reduce overall climate impact.

---

62 United Nations Framework Convention for Climate Change (2019) "Sports for Climate Action Framework," Unfcc.Int, (Accessed 10/7/2019)

3. Educate for climate action.

4. Promote sustainable and responsible consumption.

5. Advocate for climate action through communication.

UN Climate Change invites all sports organizations to sign up to the principles, "regardless of their current stage in their environmental endeavors and work collaboratively to identify and spotlight climate solutions."[63]

Dave Newport and the Pac-12 Conference's story shows that not only can fulfilling these five principles help unify sports organizations as a force for environmental good, but they are also an opportunity to attract and retain corporate sponsors.

To me, it seems that all sponsorship deals moving forward could align with this framework, and in fact, corporate sponsors in sports should sign the Climate Action framework as well. There is no downside to signing.

Taking action to combat climate change will require a great deal of resources, and corporate sponsors are already putting billions of dollars into sports to connect with consumers. What better way is there for a brand to connect with consumers than to promote sustainable and responsible consumption of their products, so that we might save our planet?

---

63 Ibid.

It is imperative that sponsors and sponsorship seekers understand and practice the principle of sustainability in their partnerships moving forward. Sponsorships can help fulfill the potential of sports and entertainment to positively stabilize the climate and promote peace and prosperity.

THREE WINS FROM CHAPTER 6

- The third principle of Three-Win sponsorship is **sustainability**. Climate change has already begun to affect the sports and entertainment industries in a negative way. Increased temperatures could force match cancellations or even force leagues to shift the timing of their seasons. Sponsors and properties have the opportunity to be a part of the solution and empower their fans to be a contributing force to climate action.
- Dave Newport's story from the University of Florida to the University of Colorado to the Pac-12 proves that *sustainability sells*. Brands want to affiliate with green consumer behavior, but it is up to the sponsorship seekers to build the sustainable business practices and infrastructure first before they can actually sell sponsorship against those assets.
- The Sustainable Development Goals and the Sports for Climate Action framework provide a blueprint for how organizations and individuals throughout the sports and entertainment industry can get involved. Leaders

should begin thinking about how to tie their core business objectives to these sustainability efforts and get their customers involved in the process. There is no downside to building more sustainable businesses, but much downside to doing nothing.

CHAPTER 7

MEASURE WHAT MATTERS

———

"We must realize—and act on the realization—that if we try to focus on everything, we focus on nothing."

—JOHN DOERR

**

What good is sponsorship, anyway, if you can't measure its impact on your business? This is one of the core questions that every sponsor and sponsee must grapple with each time they enter into a partnership.

The fact of the matter is sponsors must measure how effective their marketing dollars are at driving results for their brand, but, in the past, many sponsors have looked at measuring their portfolios all wrong.

In *The Sponsorship Seeker's Toolkit*, Kim Skildum-Reid and Anne-Marie Grey dispel the myth that sponsorship should be all about return on investment (ROI). Instead, they encourage sponsorship seekers and their sponsor partners to think more along the lines of return on objectives (ROO).

"ROO," write Skildum-Reid and Grey, "takes back the idea that sponsorship measurement is multi-faceted and based on overall marketing and business objectives."[64] They tell us that some of the most important returns that sponsorship can produce are things like:

- Shifts in consumer perception of the brand
- Increasing the loyalty or advocacy of key target markets
- Deepening of relationships with major clients
- Shifts in consumer behavior
- Consumer understanding and alignment

However, each of these outcomes have very different measures and benchmarks that are unique to every sponsorship.

64 Skildum-Reid, Kim and Anne-Marie Grey. *The Sponsorship Seeker's Toolkit, Fourth Edition.* McGraw Hill Education, 2014.

And, Skildum-Reid and Grey write, "it is the sponsor's leverage program that turns that [sponsorship] into a result against the sponsor's marketing and business objectives."

This principle is critically important as we build and execute sponsorships today, making the fourth principle for effective Three-Win sponsorship **measurement**.

To recap each of the principles thus far, when a sponsor and a sponsorship seeker come together to set up a partnership, both parties will have aligned on a common and clear **intention** as to the Third Win they plan to deliver for the target market. They will have built out a leverage plan to create value for the intended audience in an **authentic** way, which speaks to why the sponsor is becoming a part of that target market's story. And, finally, the sponsor and property will have designed activations, messaging, and incentives for the target market that foster **sustainable** behaviors to ensure they are all being good stewards of the planet.

Before they launch the sponsor partnership, however, the sponsor must identify how they plan to **measure** the outcomes for their business *and* for their target market. Don't forget—the third win is *the most important win of all*, but we must know what success looks like for our target markets. We have to track the progress we make through sponsorship activation by using benchmarks of where we started and have a clear time frame during which we will try to hit a specific target.

The good news is the sponsorship discipline has a leader already moving the industry in the direction of effective measurement of sponsorship. They are rewiring all of their sponsorships to reward great performance and outcomes and shifting their entire massive budget to their new ROO-based framework. Let's see how they're doing it.

THE BEERMAKER SHAKING UP SPONSORSHIP

Anheuser-Busch (A-B) has been the most dominant beer company in the United States for decades. Its dominance over the US beer market has likely been due to a number of factors, from the quality of its products to the strength of its brand identity to its creative and often entertaining TV advertisements.

One major contributing factor to its success has been its sponsorship strategy in the sports and entertainment space. For years, Budweiser and Bud Light, along with other A-B product logos, have been plastered all over baseball stadiums, basketball arenas, hockey rinks, and NASCAR race tracks across the country. Why? Anheuser-Busch wanted to be the beer of choice for sports fans every time they went to a game or a race.

A-B has consistently been one of the highest spenders in the US sponsorship industry. According to the 2018 Sponsorship Report from IEG, Anheuser-Busch was the second-biggest US sponsorship spender in 2016 with a $355 million spend.[65] As you might imagine, with a budget that big, when A-B decides to change the way it spends money, the entire sports and entertainment industry pays attention.

In April 2018, the beer giant did exactly that. Anheuser-Busch announced it would be rolling out a brand-new incentive-based sponsorship framework for its entire sponsorship portfolio. In an interview with Forbes, Joao Chueiri, vice president of marketing at Anheuser-Busch InBev, said the legacy way of doing sponsorship was outdated. "We need to evolve the model, and as the leaders in the industry, we are pushing for that evolution," Chueiri said.[66]

This revolutionary new model was built in a similar way to how professional athletes receive large bonuses for exceptional performance on the field of play. For example, an NFL player could have incentive-based clauses in his contract for making the Pro Bowl, being voted onto an All-Pro team, or

---

65 IEG. "What Sponsors Want & Where Dollars Will Go In 2018." Sponsorship.Com. (Accessed September 3, 2019).

66 Badenhausen, Kurt. "Anheuser-Busch Launches Revolutionary Incentive-Based Sponsorship Model". April 2, 2018. *Forbes.Com.* (Accessed October 7, 2019).

even meeting certain statistical thresholds such as a number of receiving yards or touchdowns.

The pro athlete incentive model was familiar for Joao Chueiri because he spent seven years working for Nike prior to joining A-B. He told Forbes, "Coming from the sports industry, compensation based on performance is something that is very natural."

Applying that model to sports properties, A-B decided to rewrite each of its agreements with sports teams, starting with a baseline fee and integrating incentives for great performance. The key performance indicators that could enable a team to achieve those payments, Chueiri told Sports Business Journal, included attendance, wins and losses and other on-field performance measures, social media and other fan engagement metrics, and brand awareness and consideration among those aware of the sponsorship. "The idea is to motivate the property to ensure every fan knows that Budweiser is the official beer," wrote Terry Lofton for Sports Business Journal.[67]

At the time of its announcement, Anheuser-Busch claimed it was "the first major sponsor to adopt this incentive-based model for teams and leagues."

---

67 Lofton, Terry. "A-B'S Sponsor Shocker". April 2, 2018. *Sportsbusinessdaily.Com*. (Accessed October 7, 2019).

The sports industry media coverage made it clear this model was a big deal. Sports Business Journal ran a story on the new model titled "A-B's sponsor shocker: Top U.S. sports spender rewrites sponsorship rules with new incentive-based contracts." Forbes staff writer Kurt Badenhausen wrote that the new model "promises to shake up the industry."

Another key player in Anheuser-Busch's sponsorship model is Nick Kelly, vice president of partnerships, beer culture and community at A-B InBev. During an interview with Front Office Sports CEO Adam White at the 2018 IEG Sponsorship Conference, Kelly discussed in more detail why A-B decided to move toward an incentive-based sponsorship framework.[68]

"The biggest thing is that we're all fighting for attention," Kelly said. "We're fighting for attention from consumers who have so many more choices between how they consume a property, [and] how they consume a brand. What we're trying to do with our new incentive-based model is work together in a true partnership with teams to deliver on unified goals."

Among those unified goals? Getting in front of and connecting with younger fans through social media channels and creating experiences that make fans want to come back again

---

68   Front Office Sports. "Shot Callers Episode 2: Nick Kelly, Head Of US Sports Marketing, Anheuser-Busch Inbev". May 9, 2018. *frntofficesport.com*. (Accessed October 7, 2019).

and again. In Kelly and A-B's eyes, the traditional sponsorship assets were not providing the ROO they sought, so it made sense for them to do things differently.

"We were really trying to push the envelope on how we value and quantify experiential marketing, and hopefully we're pushing the industry in a comfortable way to get to that next level," Kelly explained.

One thing Nick Kelly, Joao Chueiri, and Anheuser-Busch would like to make clear, though, is that they are not spending less money on sponsorship. They are simply spending it in a different way that aligns more closely with their business objectives.

"The traditional sponsorship model, based on fees and media commitments, does not deliver the best value for us at a time when most leagues and teams are facing challenges with live attendance and TV ratings," Chueiri told Sports Business Journal. "We want to evolve the model and encourage fan engagement … with an awareness that each deal is unique."[69]

Kelly reinforced that message by citing the success of sponsoring the 2017–2018 Super Bowl Champion Philadelphia Eagles. Fans of the Eagles truly embraced Bud Light's "Dilly

---

69 Lofton, Terry. "A-B'S Sponsor Shocker". April 2, 2018. *Sportsbusinessdaily.Com*. (Accessed October 7, 2019).

Dilly" tagline and made it their own rallying cry during the title run. Eagles fans showed up to games with "Philly Philly" signs, and a bet on Twitter with Eagles offensive lineman, Lane Johnson, forced A-B to buy forty thousand beers for the Eagles Super Bowl parade in February 2018.

"Those are the types of experiences we want to continue to push, in replacement of some of the traditional assets like signage and media," said Kelly.

When asked about the biggest pain point A-B has experienced in shifting to its new sponsorship model, Kelly referenced that properties felt a bit of pain initially, since they had always counted on Budweiser or Bud Light to sponsor traditional assets in their stadiums. Kelly told property partners, "I know there's value [in traditional assets] because I've been buying them for years, but we're going to give you this value back to go to sell somebody else. I still want to buy that same amount of value, but I want to buy it another way."

Moving forward, Anheuser-Busch will apply the incentivized sponsorship model to its portfolio in music and entertainment. "We're going to almost mirror what we're doing in sports, in music and entertainment," explained Kelly. "There should be no reason that a music festival isn't in the same conditions for sports properties because they have 100,000 people that come over a weekend or 200,000. They have the ability to engage them on a mobile app, and the ability to create content to push out on our behalf at the event."

A-B MAKES A SUSTAINABILITY STATEMENT

During the February 2019 Super Bowl between the New England Patriots and Los Angeles Rams, Anheuser-Busch continued its long-standing tradition of running television ads during the big game. While it ran commercials for several of its portfolio brands, including Michelob and Stella Artois, one ad in particular stood out as different from the others.

In a forty-five-second spot for Budweiser, featuring the famous Clydesdale horses trotting amidst wind turbines, A-B announced that Budweiser was "now brewed with wind power."

"This Bud's for a Better Tomorrow," the commercial signed off, as Bob Dylan's "Blowin' in the Wind" played in the background.

In a 2017 tweet from AB InBev's Twitter account, Anheuser-Busch InBev CEO Carlos Brito said, "Climate change is the most pressing issue confronting our planet. We at AB InBev are committed to doing our part."[70]

---

70 Anheuser-Busch InBev, Twitter Post, June 3, 2017, 8:35 AM. twitter. com/abinbev

The company set sustainability goals for itself so that by the year 2025, according to AB InBev's website[71],

- One hundred percent of its direct farmers would be skilled, connected, and financially empowered
- One hundred percent of its communities in high-stress areas will have measurably improved water quality and access.
- One hundred percent of its products will be in packaging that is returnable or made from majority recycled content.
- One hundred percent of its purchased electricity will be from renewable sources.
- There will be twenty-five percent reduction in carbon dioxide emissions across its value chain.

Anheuser-Busch, with its sustainability focused messaging during the 2019 Super Bowl, backed up by company-wide sustainability commitments, again shows us why it's important for brands to take a stand on issues that affect its customers everyday lives. However, I think its incentive-based sponsorship model provides even deeper lessons for Three-Win sponsorship practitioners—**measure and incentivize what really matters**.

---

71 Anheuser-Busch InBev. "2025 Sustainability Goals". 2019. *Ab-Inbev. Com*. Accessed October 7 2019.

MAKE IMPACT MEASURABLE

If we take A-B's incentive model a step further and apply it to the community engagement and social impact aspects of our sponsorship deals, think of the possibilities for growing the impact of sports and entertainment on people and the planet.

What if a major financial institution like Bank of America provided a chunk of its annual sponsorship of Major League Baseball for the financial literacy education of every baseball fan in America? And what if B of A incentivized MLB with additional funds for this program based upon the number of consumers reached, the number of hours spent learning, and the percentage increase in knowledge around important personal finance topics?

Imagine if Kaiser Permanente incentivized its partners at the NBA to drive mental health and well-being resources into underserved communities, to help young people cope with depression, anxiety, and other mental health challenges? It would spur the NBA and its member teams to deliver measurable solutions which could drive population-level change on an extremely stigmatized problem.

The key takeaway here is that when you are designing the Third Win in your sponsorship deals, make sure to determine the right incentives in such a way that they are measurable, so that if you are able to perform like an All-Star in the community, the sponsor and the property can be confident their dollars are being spent wisely.

**

So we've uncovered four of the five principles of effective Three-Win sponsorships: *intention, authenticity, sustainability,* and *measurement.* It feels like we have all our bases covered, right?

Not quite.

Our final principle ties everything together into a neat little bow, but, if it gets overlooked, it can ruin all of the hard work you have put in on the front end. While you may want to feel like you are under control of the success of your sponsorships, the final principle displays that if you want to really see your sponsorship results take off, you're going to have to *let go.*

THREE WINS FROM CHAPTER 7

- The fourth principle of Three-Win sponsorship is **measurement**. Sponsors and sponsees undertaking deals must set their objectives at the outset of their partnerships so that can measure the effect of the platform on their businesses and on their target markets.

- Anheuser-Busch's new incentive-based sponsorship framework provides a template for the industry to follow in order to implement measurable sponsorships. A-B sets clear, measurable objectives for its sponsor partners, which incentivize sponsees to deliver on those key outcomes in order to unlock more revenue.
- It's important to remember that measurable outcomes should be set for both the sponsor, and for the desired impact—the Third Win—for the target market. Achieving measurable wins for the target market will ensure that you can communicate an authentic success story through the sponsorship platform.

CHAPTER 8

ALL TOGETHER NOW

———

"You may say that I'm a dreamer
But I'm not the only one
I hope someday you'll join us
And the world will live as one"

−JOHN LENNON

∗∗

Toward the end of their 2018 season, Toronto FC soccer fans received a real shock when they showed up to BMO Field and were offered a free meal by stadium staff at halftime of the match. As they settled down into their seats to tuck into their food at the thirty thousand-seat stadium, a video came on the big screen.[72]

"4 million Canadians go hungry every year," the public service announcement video began. "People like Ann, battling cancer. And Gladys, and her two children."

"Every minute, Canada wastes enough food to feed a stadium," the video continued. "So, two days ago, we collected food that would've been thrown out from local grocery stores. And today, we fed that food to this stadium." Toronto FC fans, stunned, are shown holding their hands over their mouth, staring blankly at the big screen or nodding their heads in approval at the video recapping the event.

"Hellmann's and MLSE are proud to announce a new partnership," the PSA concludes. "After stadium events, we'll collect the leftover food, and give it to those in need. Each year, we'll donate 50,000 meals to the volunteers, families, and friends who need it most. That's more real food, for more real people."

At the conclusion of the video, fans were moved enough to give a standing ovation for Hellmann's and Toronto FC

---

72 Hellmann's® Canada. "Hellmann's® Feeds A Stadium Food Waste – Real Food Rescue". October 1, 2019. *Youtube*. (Accessed October 7, 2019).

successfully pulling a fast one on them but in a way that made them aware of a critical environmental issue in their country.

To me, the Hellmann's Feeds a Stadium activation is one of the best examples of a powerful, effective Three-Win sponsorship during the entire year of 2018. It checks all the boxes when it comes to the principles we've laid out in this book.

It was **intentional.** Hellmann's—a Unilever Canada food brand that makes several kinds of mayonnaise products—set out in search for a partner with whom they could raise awareness on the problem of food waste. They found that partner in Maple Leaf Sports & Entertainment, the largest sports and entertainment company in Canada, which owns several Toronto-based sports franchises, including Toronto FC.

It was **authentic.** Food waste was not an issue that was brand new to Hellmann's. In fact, they started getting involved in tackling the issue of food waste in 2007, when they launched Urban Gardens in Toronto as part of a larger platform, the Hellmann's Real Food Movement. Gina Kiroff, director of foods at Unilever Canada, told the Canadian website, *Strategy*, that "as a brand, Hellmann's has every right to play in this space," given their track record over the previous decade.

It was **sustainable.** The purpose of the "Hellmann's Feeds a Stadium" sponsorship activation was sustainable to its core!

Food waste is a massive problem that compounds many of the issues affecting our planet's environment. The activation did a great job of not only building awareness and understanding of the problem, but also taking action to address the problem.

It was **measurable**. Notice that Hellmann's used concrete numbers to define the problem—"4 million Canadians go hungry every year" and "Every minute Canada wastes enough food to feed a stadium"—and to define their goal— "Each year, we'll donate 50,000 meals to the volunteers, families, and friends who need it most." As a sponsor, Hellman's could also benchmark itself against the meals served goal, or other specific and measurable goals, such as number of views of their recap video or social media impressions.

Hellmann's and MLSE deserve high marks on all four of the principles we've revealed thus far. But the reason that it was so effective was because of its flawless execution of the fifth principle: **ownership**.

LET YOUR FANS DO THE MARKETING

You see, the whole reason brands get involved with sponsorship in the first place is to connect in a genuine way with a target audience and convince their audience that their brand is the obvious choice. After all of these years, and all of the different phases of sponsorship that we have gone through, this is still the primary objective of sponsorship in the sports and entertainment world.

And yet, you can still see brands and properties executing sponsorships that forget the critically important fact that, "the third win is the most important win of all," as Kim Skildum-Reid taught us earlier. To put it another way, sponsorship is all about bringing value to the target audience, so that those people remember your brand and choose your brand going forward.

Hellmann's and its partners over at MLSE/Toronto FC understood this. And the success of its sponsorship exemplifies why it is so important to bring the target audience into the sponsorship and make them feel a part of the story. Even better, they showed Toronto FC fans that *they* could be a part of the solution to the food waste problem and created a microsite for ongoing tips and tricks to participate in lowering food waste.

Sponsorship can only reach its full potential when the target audience is engaged and feels ownership over the activation. Sponsors and properties must make the target audience engaged to the point where they feel like they have a vested interest in the sponsorship. By now, I hope you realize that integrating social impact into sponsorships is a fantastic way to get your target audience invested and engaged.

The stories we've covered in this book demonstrate that the most effective sponsorships in the industry are the ones in which consumers are actively involved in the sponsorship and feel like they are the key to the sponsorship's success. Let's review how a few of them exemplify the importance of **ownership** in Three-Win sponsorships.

- T-Mobile's Home Runs for Hurricane Recovery campaign, through its sponsorship platform with MLB, was so successful because it made fans' actions—the hundreds of thousands of tweets sent out by MLB fans in support of #HR4HR—the key to the success of the campaign. Ultimately, it was because of the fans' support on Twitter that T-Mobile was able to contribute over $2.5 million in hurricane relief funds to Team Rubicon. I remember Tweeting out #HR4HR myself during the 2017 MLB postseason, and I recall it felt pretty darn good.
- US Bank's sponsorship portfolio was completely revamped after it started working with Ania Sponaski and GMR Marketing. Its focus shifted toward community engagement with all of its activations, because that was what it heard was "most important" to its customers. The Charlotte Rail Trail sponsorship goes to show that a brand doesn't have to just sponsor traditional sports and entertainment assets, either. If you listen to your target markets, they will tell you what is important to them and what value your brand can bring to their lives.

- By standing with Colin Kaepernick for its "Just Do It" anniversary campaign, Nike made it clear to the world it believed in the causes that Kaepernick fought for, specifically, Black Lives Matter and that police brutality and unjust violence against people of color must end. Nike could've taken a step further and taken action to empower people in these movements, but if you were a person of color fighting for an end to police brutality during the year 2018, and you saw the Nike-Kaepernick campaign, you must have felt a certain assurance that a big brand like Nike had your back and supported your cause.

- The entire purpose of the University of Colorado, Boulder's Ralphie's Green Stampede platform was to encourage sustainable behaviors by their fans at home, work, and play. Yes, it was building out sponsorships in a way that checks all of the boxes for the other four principles, but none those elements would have mattered unless it brought its fans into the equation as the ultimate owners of the sponsorship. Dave Newport taught us that brands like Wells Fargo are lining up to be associated with fostering sustainable fan behavior.

- Gillette has only just begun its efforts to foster positive masculinity through its "The Best Men Can Be" initiative, but the company did pledge $1 million dollars per year over three years "to non-profit organizations executing the most interesting and impactful programs designed to **help men of all ages achieve their personal best."** It will be interesting to see whether the brand leverages its naming rights sponsorship of the New England Patriots stadium to further its message of male leadership, advocacy, and mentorship of the next generation.

As we enter the year 2020, a new decade brings feelings of hope and possibility. Unfortunately, it will also bring all of the big, hairy problems that we have been facing in our world throughout the twenty-first century.

While the problems aren't going away, there are shining examples across the entire sports and entertainment sponsorship world that show how leading with purpose and social impact can change consumers hearts and minds.

The 2020s will also bring a whole new set of massive sporting events to North America. We have a tremendous opportunity in front of us in the coming years to change the way we approach sponsorships so that we might **both** connect better with consumers **and** inspire a whole generation of people to make the world a better, safer, more peaceful place.

Before we close, let's take a look at some of the opportunities ahead in the 2020s, and leverage the five principles of Three-Win sponsorships to explore ways we might apply them going forward.

In Part 3, we will examine the path forward from the perspective of talent, properties, and brands. Each have a role to play in implementing Three-Win sponsorship methodology so that we might transform the way business is done in the industry.

THREE WINS FROM CHAPTER 8

- The fifth principle of effective Three-Win sponsorship is **ownership**. It is perhaps the most important principle to understand and put into practice.
- Hellman's and Toronto FC's "Hellman's Feeds a Stadium" activation displays the importance of making your target market feel ownership over the success of the sponsorship.
- Sponsorship deals will only reach their true potential when the brands and properties or talent get the target market deeply engaged with the success of the partnership.

PART THREE

THE QUARTERBACK, THE PLAYING FIELD, AND THE FANS

CHAPTER 9

THE QUARTERBACK

———

"A life is not important except in the impact it has on other lives."

—JACKIE ROBINSON

**

You may be thinking after reading Parts 1 and 2: what role should I or my organization play in the shift toward Three-Win sponsorship? That is the core question we'll aim to answer in Part 3.

I want to make this as actionable for readers as possible, so we'll examine the role that talent, properties, and brands can play to usher in this new phase of purpose-driven marketing in sports and entertainment.

To do so, let's imagine for a minute that the entire sports and entertainment industry is playing one big game of (American) football.

On any given Sunday, there are dozens of different roles that need to be played in order for the game to happen. There are players, coaches, referees, front office management, broadcasters, reporters, vendors, and fans. Each role serves a different purpose in executing the game and making sure everything runs smoothly.

In a similar sense, talent, properties, and brands all play a different role in executing the business side of the industry. The athletes, artists, and entertainers are the draw. They are the reason that we tune in or buy tickets. We want to witness their brilliance on the field, court, or stage. We want to be inspired, shocked, or enraged. Talent leads and drives everything else in the industry.

In our football game analogy, **talent** is **The Quarterback**. It is the most recognizable leader in the industry. Talent gets all of the praise when things go well and the majority of the blame when things go poorly. On top of that, talent often leads society on important global issues. There are countless examples of activist athletes, actors, and musicians who "quarterback" big social and environmental issues around the world.

Quarterbacks have influence, and the very best quarterbacks use their influence to lift up the rest of their teammates, inspiring them to perform to the absolute best of their abilities. In the coming decade, the top talent from across sports and entertainment will do the same with respect to big, important causes.

**

Don't tell professional athletes to "shut up and dribble." History shows us that athletes are often among the most courageous and impactful change agents in the world.

From Jackie Robinson breaking the color barrier in Major League Baseball for the Brooklyn Dodgers in the 1940s to Muhammad Ali's protest of the Vietnam War to John Carlos and Tommie Smith's Black Power salute during the 1968 Olympics at the height of the Civil Rights Movement, there are incredible examples of how professional athletes have fought for causes bigger than their sport.

As we saw in Chapter 5, athletes like Colin Kaepernick have carried the torch of athlete activism in the twenty-first century. However, as we look ahead at the next decade, athlete activism will continue to grow.

We already see how athletes are leading the charge, so let's look specifically at how female athletes have been using their platforms and support from their corporate sponsors to fight for issues bigger than themselves.

ALLYSON FELIX AND WOMEN'S EMPOWERMENT

It's not often that Nike loses one of its signature endorsement athletes to a competitor. So when Allyson Felix left Nike to sign an endorsement deal with Gap-owned women's athletic apparel brand Athleta in August 2019, marketers across the business world payed attention.

How did Nike lose Felix, one of the most accomplished Olympic sprinters of all time, to Athleta? For that matter, why did Felix choose Athleta over Nike and all of the other major apparel brands she could have worked with?

It all started with Felix penning a courageous op-ed in The New York Times on May 22, 2019, titled "Allyson Felix: My Own Nike Pregnancy Story."

In her opinion piece, Felix tells the story of her sponsorship deal with Nike and how she and her fellow female athletes risk pay cuts from the company during pregnancy and afterwards. "It's one example of a sports industry where the rules are still mostly made for and by men," Felix wrote.[73]

She went on to share how, in 2018, she decided to start a family while at the same time negotiating a renewal of her endorsement deal with Nike. At thirty-two, Felix was a six-time Olympic gold medal winner, and an eleven-time world champion sprinter. However, negotiations with Nike were not going well for her—the company wanted to pay her seventy percent less than before.

"I felt pressure to return to form as soon as possible after the birth of my daughter in November 2018, even though I ultimately had to undergo an emergency C-section at 32 weeks because of severe pre-eclampsia that threatened the lives of me and my baby," Felix explained.

Felix and her team asked Nike to include a guarantee in her new contract that she would not be punished for decreased performance in the ensuing months after the birth of her child.

"I wanted to set a new standard. If I, one of Nike's most widely marketed athletes, couldn't secure these protections, who could?" she wrote in The New York Times.

---

73 Felix, Allyson. "Opinion: My Own Nike Pregnancy Story". *The New York Times,* May 22, 2019. *Nytimes.Com.* Accessed October 7 2019.

Nike declined to include the clause in the contract, and negotiations came to a halt.

Felix shared the irony in the situation she found herself in with Nike. When she first met with the company's leadership in 2010, a woman had sold her on integration into a Nike-sponsored initiative called the Girl Effect, which "promoted adolescent girls as the key to improving societies around the world." Felix believed that by endorsing Nike, she could help empower women and girls.

But her experience around her pregnancy and her contract renewal made her realize she needed to take a stand to truly inspire and impact women and girls around the world.

To Nike's credit, it acted quickly after Felix and two of her former teammates spoke out to change their maternity policy and announced that "it is adding language to new contracts for female athletes that will protect their pay during pregnancy." But, in the end, it was not enough to renew Felix's contract.

Athleta moved quickly to swoop in and sign Allyson Felix to an endorsement deal on July 31, 2019. Felix became the brand's first-ever athlete endorser and the core piece to a relaunch of Athleta's "Power of She" marketing platform.

Speaking with PEOPLE magazine after the Athleta deal was announced, Felix said "I'm just really thrilled about it. The way that they are doing sponsorship to me is incredible. It is focused on me as a whole—as an athlete, as a mom, and as an activist and just to be supported in that way is amazing."[74]

Athleta's CMO Sheila Shekar Pollak told Forbes the brand had a long-standing commitment to women's issues, saying "Athleta has been at the forefront of empowering and celebrating women for two decades and the brand has always stood for the empowerment of women and inspiring the next generation of girls through sport."[75]

"We are a purpose-driven brand and everything we create and do is in service of our mission to empower a community of active, healthy, confident women and girls." Pollak continued. Athleta has contributed to several initiatives including partnerships with the Movemeant Foundation and Girls Leadership, both of which support helping girls grow and gain confidence.

---

74 Evans, Morgan M. "Olympic Sprinter Allyson Felix Has a New Partnership That's Championing Female Athletes and Mothers" *PEOPLE*, July 31, 2019. people.com. (Accessed October 7, 2019).

75 Taylor, Charles. "Why The Allyson Felix And Athleta Partnership Will Work." *Forbes*, August 7, 2019. Forbes.com. (Accessed October 7, 2019).

The Allyson Felix and Athleta partnership was a perfect fit because of shared values. As Felix told Forbes, "When I met with the team at Athleta, there was an immediate connection of values. They're champions of women and girls. They're truly invested in me as more than just an athlete – but as a woman, a mother and an activist. I'm really looking forward to what we can create together."

USWNT'S FIGHT FOR EQUAL PAY

Athlete leadership and activism on progressive social issues has also played out in a team setting in recent years, with the U.S. Women's National Soccer Team (USWNT) being the most prominent example.

In 2016, one year after their team's triumph at the 2015 World Cup, five USWNT players—Alex Morgan, Megan Rapinoe, Becky Sauerbrunn, Carli Lloyd, and Hope Solo—filed a wage discrimination complaint with the Equal Employment Opportunity Commission (EEOC) citing that women's team players are paid significantly less than their men's team counterparts. This complaint became the first step in an ongoing fight for equal pay between the USWNT and U.S. Soccer Federation (USSF).[76]

---

76   ESPN News Services. "USWNT suing U.S. Soccer for discrimination." ESPN.com, March 8, 2019. Accessed October 7, 2019

The EEOC complaint became a bargaining chip that the USWNT Player's Association used to negotiate a new Collective Bargaining Agreement (CBA) with U.S. Soccer in 2017. However, the players continued to experience significant gaps in pay and working conditions.

Then, in March 2019, as they geared up for the 2019 World Cup, twenty-eight members of the team sued U.S. Soccer in federal court accusing the federation of years of institutionalized gender discrimination.

"Despite the fact that these female and male players are called upon to perform the same job responsibilities on their teams and participate in international competitions for their single common employer, the USSF, the female players have been consistently paid less money than their male counterparts," the lawsuit said. "This is true even though their performance has been superior to that of the male players – – with the female players, in contrast to male players, becoming world champions."

One of the co-captains of the squad, Megan Rapinoe, told ESPN at the time, "I don't know if there was a tipping point, but the feeling was that this was the next best step for us to put us in the best possible position to continue to fight for what we believe is right and what the law recognizes. And to try to achieve equality under the law, equal working conditions, equal working pay. It goes far beyond equal pay into the working conditions as well."[77]

"We believe it is our duty to be the role models that we've set out to be and fight for what we know we legally deserve," forward Christen Press told The Associated Press. "And hopefully in that way it inspires women everywhere."

While there was complexity and nuance to the issue of equal pay between the men's and women's soccer teams, including the fact that the teams brokered separate Collective Bargaining Agreements with the USSF, one clear disparity in compensation was the bonuses paid by FIFA to teams that participated in the World Cup. On that front, men's teams were paid bonuses more than ten times higher than women's clubs by the global governing body.

So which side did the sponsors land on? Overwhelmingly, sponsors backed the USWNT players.

LUNA Bar, a protein and energy bar brand owned by Clif Bar & Company, announced in late March 2019 that they would help fill the gap between the roster bonuses received by the US men's and women's squads by donating $31,250 to each

---

77 Ibid.

of the twenty-three women who made the World Cup team via their Players' Association.

"It's ironic that one of the most popular sports in the world is still experiencing pay inequalities between women and men," said Clif Bar & Company Owner and Co-CEO Kit Crawford in a press release. "We are big fans of the U.S. Women's National Team and were inspired to take action and make a difference that matters. LUNA Bar is honored to give these women, and women everywhere, our support. It's what is right, but more importantly, it's what they deserve."[78]

"When LUNA Bar approached us in January to support and recognize the USWNT players in this way, I was speechless," said USWNTPA Executive Director Becca Roux. "Many brands raising awareness for equal pay use the USWNT's fight as an example, but don't go the extra step to offer a solution to the problem. LUNA Bar has a long history of supporting women's equality and is truly walking the walk by maximizing the amount of money going directly to the players and intentionally closing one of their pay gaps."

In addition to LUNA, Procter & Gamble (P&G) leaned into the issue and sided with the women's team. After the women's

---

78 BusinessWire. "LUNA® Bar Moves U.S. Women'S National Soccer Team One Step Closer To Equal Pay". *Businesswire.Com*, April 2, 2019. (Accessed October 7, 2019).

team was crowned World Cup Champions once again in July 2019, P&G took out a full-page ad in The New York Times urging the USSF, of whom P&G was an official sponsor, to be "on the right side of history" with respect to the team's equal pay fight.[79]

Through P&G's deodorant brand Secret, the company announced it would make a $529,000 donation to the USWNTPA, equal to $23,000 for each of the team's twenty-three members.

During an appearance on *Meet the Press*, Rapinoe discussed the role that sponsors like LUNA and P&G can play in their fight. "These are some of the most powerful corporations, not just in sports but in the world, and have so much weight that they can throw around," she said. "And I think that they just need to get comfortable with throwing it around."

Roux weighed in as well, "For brands, and especially a brand that is also a U.S. soccer sponsor, to support our players both financially and publicly is hugely significant and important. Equity and pay equity are systemic issues that need systemic

---

79 Das, Andrew. "U.S. Soccer Sponsor Enters Equal Pay Fight On Women'S Side". 2019. *The New York Times,* July 14, 2019. *Nytimes.Com.* (Accessed October 7, 2019).

solutions. Corporations are powerful, influential players within the system that can spur massive change for good."

✶✶

Muhammad Ali summed up the power of his platform as one of the greatest athletes in the world during an interview in the 1970s. "[When] one man of popularity can let the world know about the problem, he might lose a few dollars himself telling the truth. He might lose his life. But he's helping millions. If I kept my mouth shut just because I can make millions, then this ain't doin' nothing. So I just love the freedom and the flesh and blood of my people more than I do the money."

The wave of athlete activism has yet to crest. Rather, it appears to only be gaining momentum. Everyone in the sports and entertainment industry will play some role in the shift toward Three-Win sponsorship methodology. However, it begins with leadership from transcendent talent, from men and women of popularity, standing up and telling the truth about a problem.

As opposed to the environment that Ali lived through in the '60s and '70s, in which he risked his life and risked millions of dollars by speaking truth to power, athletes in this generation and beyond have an opportunity to shine light on a problem *and* make millions in the process. Doing good is finally becoming good business for athletes, artists, and entertainers across the world.

In the 2020s, we will continue to see brands like Athleta, LUNA, and Procter & Gamble throwing their weight around to support and amplify the voices of activist athletes. However, it will be up to the next generation of talent to pick up where Allyson Felix, Megan Rapinoe, and Colin Kaepernick have left off.

THREE WINS FROM CHAPTER 9

- As the Third Win movement begins to pick up steam, we are seeing that talent will be the leaders of this shift toward purpose-driven sponsorship. Iconic figures such as Jackie Robinson and Muhammad Ali laid the foundation for athletes today to carry the torch and speak truth about big social issues.
- In 2019, we saw female athletes including Allyson Felix and members of the US Women's National Soccer Team step into leading roles on social issues affecting women in the United States and internationally. Following their lead, sponsors "threw their weight around" on those issues by offering their public support and financial resources to their cause.

- We will continue to see athletes and talent in the sports and entertainment industry take stands on important social and environmental issues. Brands can benefit by publicly supporting talent on unifying issues that affect society and, in particular, their target markets.

CHAPTER 10

THE PLAYING FIELD

—

"Where else do we dream of defeating our heroes?
Where else do you fight for more than a win?
Where else is an injury just the beginning?
Where else is a mountain no match for a 10-year old?
Where else is standing up the bravest thing you can do?
Where else does a walk-on become the MVP?
There's no place like sports."

—ESPN

**

Assuming talent in the sports and entertainment industry will be the leading voices and faces of the Third Win movement—The Quarterback—where does that leave the leagues, teams, and venues where these individuals perform? What role do properties have to play in this story?

Continuing our football game analogy from Chapter 9, properties can play the role of **The Playing Field**.

Properties serve as the platform upon which our heroes perform. They provide history, record books, and iconic fields of play. They help to stoke rivalries in sports, and they serve as the venue for memorable moments across generations of fans. Properties also provide a platform for brands to tell stories and connect with consumers.

When companies consider ways to break through to consumers in a specific region, one of the first things they likely consider is "What are our target market's favorite teams? Who do they root for? Where do they go to games?"

Because of fans' emotional attachment to leagues, teams, players, and artists, properties have the attention of a large group of people. With all of those eyeballs, and all of that emotion, it should not come as a surprise that advertising and marketing dollars will pour in.

With all of that financial power comes a responsibility. In my view, not only should properties serve as the platform for our athletes and artists to perform, but they also should serve as a core platform, or playing field, upon which we inspire, unite, and engage society around important issues.

How might this play out in practice throughout the next decade? Well, there are two global sports and entertainment events coming to North America during the 2020s that could provide a template for all other properties. Let's take a look at how the 2026 World Cup and the 2028 Summer Olympics might help shape the role of properties in the world of sponsorship.

**

On September 17, 2017, at the 131st International Olympic Committee (IOC) Session in Lima, Peru, the city of Los Angeles was awarded the bid to host the 2028 Summer Olympics. It set the stage for the Summer Olympics to return to the United States for the first time since the 1996 Games in Atlanta, and positioned LA as the first US city to host the Olympics three times, in 1932, 1984, and 2028.

LA 2028's successful bid committee was led by Casey Wasserman, founder of the sports marketing and talent management agency, Wasserman, and he was named chairman of the Los Angeles Olympic Organizing Committee. By taking up that role, Wasserman and the LAOOC signed up for what

Sports Business Journal has called, "the largest single sponsorship sales effort in American sports history."[80]

Their mission? To sell $2.5 billion worth of domestic sponsorship deals.

Complicating the LAOOC's revenue goal is the fact that they will compete for sponsorship dollars with the 2026 FIFA World Cup, which will take place in the United States, Canada, and Mexico, as part of a three-nation bid that FIFA awarded in 2018.

Plus, the IOC holds the rights to sell global sponsorship categories, leaving some of the largest multinational corporations off the table for Wasserman and his team.

One cannot help but look at the 2028 LA Summer Olympics and see the parallels between this future event and the 1984 LA Summer Olympics, forty-four years prior. The question is whether Casey Wasserman will be able to match the remarkable success and enduring legacy of the job that Peter Ueberroth did for LA84.

---

80 Fischer, Ben and Terry Lofton. "Gold standard," *Sports Business Journal*, October 29, 2018. sportsbusinessdaily.com (Accessed October, 7 2019)

Leaving those two men and their legacies aside for a minute, I think the more important question is whether LA 2028 will be able to meet and exceed the incredible legacy of social good that LA84 was able to create for generations to come.

APPLYING THIRD WIN PRINCIPLES TO THE 2026 WORLD CUP AND LA 2028

In my estimation, the decade of the 2020s presents a golden opportunity for the industry to shift toward purpose-driven Three-Win sponsorship. With both the FIFA World Cup coming to North America in 2026 and the Summer Olympics returning to LA in 2028, massive amounts of sponsorship dollars will be pouring into this part of the world. It is imperative that we seize this opportunity to leverage the platform that sports provides and help to address the biggest, most intractable issues facing the planet.

Recall that LA84 revolutionized Olympic marketing and sponsorship marketing and more or less saved the Olympic movement. There is reason for optimism that history will repeat itself in LA 2028, but Wasserman and the leaders of the LAOOC must be intentional about tapping into the massive resources they are pursuing for these games and ensure that a large proportion of them will be earmarked for solving social and environmental problems in the United States and across the world.

How might the 2026 World Cup and LA 2028 organizers apply the principles in this book to their ongoing sponsorship sales efforts for the next several years? Let's take a look at each event and brainstorm a few ideas.

UNITED 2026 FIFA WORLD CUP

For the first time ever, the FIFA World Cup will have three host nations rather than the traditional single host nation that FIFA has used throughout World Cup history. The United States, Canada, and Mexico's joint bid for the World Cup makes for a great story around uniting North America to celebrate "the beautiful game" in 2026. At the same time, there are likely to be challenges faced by the organizing committee to unite around a single mission and purpose for the event.

In order to confront those complex challenges, I have three recommendations for the organizing and sponsorship sales teams to implement concepts from the Three-Win sponsorship framework and ensure both financial and social good outcomes are achieved by the North American World Cup.

1) **Intention**—I recommend the 2026 World Cup organizers take a page out of Pat Gallagher, Stephanie Martin, and Neill Duffy's playbook from the Super Bowl 50 Organizing Committee and create a common purpose for the event that all three host nations can rally around and make a difference in.

At the beginning of 2020, I would like to see a joint statement from President of Canada Soccer Steven Reed, President of Federación Mexicana de Fútbol Asociación Decio De Maria, and President of the USSF Carlos Cordeiro announcing a core social purpose for the event that all three nations are getting behind. In this announcement, the United Bid Committee could announce that twenty-five percent of the sponsorship funds they raise from corporations will go toward high-performing nonprofits and enterprises promoting youth participation in sport, environmental stewardship, and diversity, equity, and inclusion.

2) **Sustainability**—CU Boulder's Ralphie's Green Stampede campaign and Pac-12 Team Green platform have taught us that sustainability sells. The 2026 World Cup should borrow the template that Dave Newport has built and apply it to its sponsorship deals, encouraging soccer fans in North America and around the world to live more sustainably at home, work, and play.

Star players from each host nation's team can begin activating these sponsorships right away by asking American, Canadian, and Mexican fans to take a pledge, just like Water for the West, via their social media accounts.

Imagine Christian Pulisic asking every single young American soccer fan to take the #GreenGoal2026 pledge through his Twitter and Instagram account! And by the way, thank you to U.S. soccer's presenting sponsor, Volkswagen, which is driving sustainability across the world with its newest electronic vehicles. I want you to steal this idea from me, U.S. soccer and Volkswagen. Just do it!!!

3) **Ownership**—Soccer fans globally draw incredible amounts of pride, joy, and emotion from cheering on their national teams in the World Cup. It would be a mistake if sponsors and the United 2026 sponsorship sales team neglected to get these fans actively engaged and bought in to the activation of these sponsorships.

This area is one in which sponsors will have to get very creative and adjust on the fly as culture and technology change between now and the actual event in the middle of the next decade. Sponsors that are looking to engage with Gen Z consumers—and what sponsor isn't—who will be coming of age and entering the workforce during this time period should familiarize themselves with new social network platforms like TikTok, which allows users to create fifteen-second videos and share with the public on a simple smartphone application.

I envision the World Cup 2026 creating a TikTok video competition that taps into young fans for creative ideas on how to conserve water at the World Cup. The winning submission could be awarded a scholarship grant to attend a university or start their own business in a science and technology field.

LA 2028 SUMMER OLYMPICS

I've outlined the stakes for the LAOOC above, but what would I tell Casey Wasserman if I were to sit down with him for a strategy session on the LA 2028 games? Heed the lessons from LA84, pick up the torch from Peter Ueberroth, and make LA 2028 an even more transformational event for the city of Los Angeles, the United States, and the world.

If Wasserman and his team do end up meeting or exceeding their $2.5 billion domestic sponsorship goal, they will have pulled off one of the great sponsorship sales projects in US history. While a great deal of those revenue dollars will be utilized in the execution of the 2028 Summer Olympics, if the LAOOC earmarks just five percent of the gross sponsorship revenue for social and environmental good investments, it would be unlocking $125 million to invest in the betterment of society and the planet.

What principles might the LAOOC apply as they take on the herculean task of raising $2.5 billion in sponsorship for LA 2028? Well, all five of them, ideally, but here are three concrete ideas for the team to apply:

1) **Authenticity**—In Chapter 5, we discussed why this principle is so important and what it actually means in the context of sponsorship, namely, that long-term consistency with your brand purpose helps you connect better with consumers, who are more powerful and more discerning than ever in the twenty-first century.

In what ways could the LA 2028 team maintain continuity in the story of the Olympics in Los Angeles? First, I would commit one percent—$25 million—of all gross sponsorship revenue to the LA84 Foundation, which was created with surplus event revenue in the aftermath of the 1984 games to sustain a legacy of social good and has since become a "nationally recognized leader in support of youth sport programs and public education about the role of sports in positive youth development."

What better way to connect the histories of two landmark Olympic Games in LA than to continue the tradition of serving millions of young people and their families in Southern California and across the United States?

In addition to granting money to the trusted philanthropic stewards at LA84 Foundation, I propose that the LAOOC commit four percent of gross sponsorship revenues—an estimated $100 million—to create The LA 2028 Social Enterprise Investment Fund. With this fund, LA 2028 could build its legacy through venture capital investments into mission-driven social impact businesses.

Entrepreneurship has always been central to the American story, and $100 million could go a long way toward jump-starting dozens of new businesses in the late 2020s and into the early 2030s.

2) **Measurement**—By the time we arrive in the summer of 2028, we will be eighteen short months away from 2030. The year 2030 is significant because it is the target year for fulfillment of the UN Sustainable Development Goals (SDGs). The 2030 Agenda for Sustainable Development was signed by every United Nations member state in 2015 to provide a "shared blueprint for peace and prosperity for people and the planet, now and into the future." Within this agreement were seventeen SDGs "which are an urgent call for action by all countries – developed and developing – in a global partnership." SDGs included ending poverty, hunger, and inequality, while improving health and well-being, education, and tackling climate change.

It seems to me that the LAOOC could align its core purpose with the UN SDGs and begin activating with partners and Olympic athletes from 2020 to 2028 to contribute to and build awareness of the SDGs. Sports Business Journal has suggested that the key to reaching $2.5 billion will be building new sellable assets, "Inventing events and other assets that can be sold and activated along the way to 2028."[81]

If I were Casey Wasserman, I would assign one or two SDGs to each of my sponsorship salespeople and build sponsorship packages with major American brands like Google, Amazon, Facebook, and Netflix that focus on addressing those goals. Then, in the lead-up to the games, Olympic athletes can be the spokespeople and storytellers on how and why the LA 2028 games and corporate sponsors are tackling each of these issues.

I would like to see a campaign for the fifth SDG, gender equality, with Katie Ledecky and Simone Biles headlining the activation and Google investing the sponsorship dollars. Make it happen, Casey!!!

3) **Ownership**—Saving the most important principle for last, I would say it is vital that the LAOOC ensures that citizens of Los Angeles, and of the entire United States, for that matter, feel like they have skin in the 2028 games. So here comes a radical idea that will enable any American to become a stakeholder in the first Summer Olympics in the United States since 1996: crowdfunding.

---

81   Ibid.

I recommend Wasserman and the LAOOC borrow from the likes of Kickstarter and Indiegogo and sell shares in the 2028 Summer Olympics Games. Suspend disbelief for a moment and pretend the IOC would be onboard with this idea and that it is even feasible within the laws of the United States. How incredible would it be for Americans to be able to buy into the success of LA 2028 and come together to fund the next generation of entrepreneurs and leaders for our country?

As part of the LA 2028 Social Enterprise Investment Fund, if I were leading the LAOOC, I would make 100 million shares available for sale to the American public for one dollar per share. I would set a ceiling of 2,500 to 5,000 shares for any one individual or household to ensure broad availability and equal access to shares for US citizens. Shareholders from across America would double the size of the LA 2028 SEI Fund and be quite literally bought into the success of the event and the success of the entrepreneurs born out of the investment fund.

Crowdfunding the Olympics wouldn't be about helping Americans save for retirement. To me, it would be a way of building upon the model built during LA84 and revolutionizing the way sporting events, sponsorships, and consumers interact. Just imagine the lessons that could be taught to young people through the issuance of a single share in the LA 2028 games to a child in their formative years.

It may be a far-fetched, outlandish idea, but I'd venture to say the LAOOC and Legends sponsorship teams are looking for all kinds of innovative ideas to reach their $2.5 billion revenue goal. Whether they launch a crowdfunding campaign or not, the LA 2028 team must find ways to get Americans of all ages interested, engaged, and involved in the Olympics. The entire world will be watching, and the way we execute LA 2028 may very well have a ripple effect on the Olympic movement for over forty years, just like LA84.

LEVERAGING A POWERFUL PLATFORM FOR GOOD

Sports and entertainment provide a global platform with which we can reach billions of people around the world. Where is the downside in using that platform for good?

Whether you are working with a large global event like the FIFA World Cup or the Olympic Games, you have an opportunity to positively impact fans and move the planet forward. Recognizing the importance and the power of that platform is the first step toward using sponsorship resources to address issues that are meaningful to your communities.

By embracing the role of "The Playing Field," properties can both develop deeper connections with their fans and communities and also stand to grow their businesses. That part of the equation leads us to our final chapter. We'll look at the core question of "What role should I play?" but from the perspective of the brands.

THREE WINS FROM CHAPTER 10

- Properties such as pro sports leagues, teams, stadiums, and arenas serve as the platform—**The Playing Field**—upon which the drama and excitement of sports and entertainment play out. They also have an opportunity to serve as the platform for rallying fans around critical social and environmental issues faced throughout the next decade.

- The 2026 FIFA World Cup and 2028 LA Summer Olympics will be two of the largest properties in North American sports history. The leaders and organizers of those events should start thinking about ways to apply Three-Win methodology to their sponsorship sales process. It will require collaborative, creative ideas for each property to achieve its revenue goals.

- There is great power and responsibility that comes with leading a sports and entertainment property in the twenty-first century. Properties who embrace the role as a platform for spreading social good will continue to grow and build deeper relationships with their fans and their communities.

CHAPTER 11

THE FANS

——

"There is no going back. The old models for business—with business running the show and consumers and employees coming along for the ride—no longer speak to the needs, longings, and practical realities of our modern society."

–ANNE BAHR THOMPSON

**

We've established that talent will play the role of **The Quarterback** in the ongoing Three-Win sponsorship movement, inspiring and leading society forward on big, important social and environmental issues. We have also examined how properties have the opportunity to be the platform, or

The Playing Field, for stories to be told and action to be taken on these issues.

But what about brands? How do they fit into the big football game that is the sports and entertainment industry?

Football games would not happen without the fans. Fans willingly invest their time, money, and energy into cheering on their teams. They support their favorite players and teams because of the sense of community and the ability to connect with other people and to feel emotions—both good and bad—that come from supporting sports teams and players.

In the grand scheme of the sports and entertainment industry, corporate brands are a lot like these fans. They voluntarily invest resources into athletes, teams, stadiums, and events. By putting their names and logos alongside talent and properties, they are saying "We are fans of this athlete/team/arena."

Brands use sponsorship to communicate to a target audience that they love the same things the target audience loves. In many ways, sponsorship is a way for a brand to *integrate itself* into a fan base and say, "We are just like you."

To take this idea a step further, brand marketers are at their best when they are playing a cheerleader or fan type of role.

Rather than pointing out how great they—the brand—are, they talk about how great the team, the players, and the fans are. They say, "look at what *we* accomplished," not "look at what *I* accomplished."

In this new era of purpose-driven marketing, brands must understand that their sponsorships should not be utilized as a way to show off how great their product or service is. The whole purpose of utilizing Three-Win sponsorship methodology is to connect with a target market, promote the target market, and support the causes of the target market.

Brands must show that they are *fans of the fans*, and they can do that by focusing on providing value to fans throughout their sponsorship platforms.

Kim Skildum-Reid hammers this point home in *The Corporate Sponsorship Toolkit* when she describes sponsorship as a discipline with "one mission, and two objectives."[82]

"Your job as a sponsor – your job as a marketer – is not to make people part of your brand story. It is to make your brand a part of your target markets' stories. Your job is to understand them and demonstrate how your brand fits with their functional, and even better, emotional needs. It's to

---

82 Skildum-Reid, Kim. *The Corporate Sponsorship Toolkit: Using sponsorship to help people fall in love with your brand* . Freya Press, 2012.

demonstrate an alignment with your customers' and potential customers' priorities and motivations."

The mission, Skildum-Reid writes, "is to get on that unconscious list of brands that are loved and trusted by your target markets. You want to be the brand that makes your target markets feel understood, valued and respected."

Along with that mission, the two objectives fall under the category of either:

1) Changing your target markets' perceptions of your brand, or

2) Changing your target markets' behaviors around your brand.

As we've explored throughout this book, brands are not going to become beloved by customers by using the old model of sponsorship. So how might a brand take the Three-Win sponsorship model and apply it to their portfolio today?

Let's examine how the naming rights sponsor of a brand new, five billion-dollar stadium could apply Three-Win principles to its leverage plan.

THE NFL IN LOS ANGELES

The National Football League has a dynamic, roller coaster history with the city of Los Angeles, California. In 1946, the Cleveland Rams were relocated to LA and played in the Los Angeles Memorial Coliseum until 1979. The Rams then moved to a new stadium in nearby Anaheim in 1980.

In 1982, the Oakland Raiders moved from the Bay Area to join the Rams in Southern California and take their place playing in the Coliseum. However, the massive 1994 Northridge earthquake did significant damage to the Coliseum and forced the Raiders back to its original home in Oakland. The Rams also left leading up to the 1995 season, deciding to make St. Louis, Missouri, its new home.

LA went from zero NFL franchises to two teams and then back to zero in the stretch of about fifty years. The NFL's drought in the City of Angels would last for twenty-one years until the St. Louis Rams and its ownership group led by Stan Kroenke decided to move the Rams back to LA.

Then suddenly, in 2017, Los Angeles found itself with two NFL teams once again, when the San Diego Chargers packed its bags and shipped its franchise north about one hundred miles to become the Los Angeles Chargers.

Perhaps the second largest media market in the United States was always destined to host two NFL teams, and, starting in the fall of 2020, those two teams will call a brand new, state-of-the-art football stadium their home.

APPLYING THREE-WIN PRINCIPLES TO SOFI STADIUM

The Los Angeles Stadium and Entertainment District at Hollywood Park (LASED) is a massive development project undertaken by LA Rams owner Stan Kroenke, covering 298 acres of mixed-use space, including retail, commercial office space, a hotel, residential units, outdoor park spaces, and a seventy thousand-seat pro football stadium at the center of it all.

With a project this big, and two high-profile NFL teams calling LASED home for decades to come, it's not surprising that the new stadium was able to land a record-breaking naming rights sponsorship deal.

Online personal finance company SoFi did the honors by committing to a twenty-year sponsorship worth a rumored thirty million dollars per year to rename LASED as SoFi Stadium.[83] Not only did the young company put its name

---

83   Soshnick, Scott. "Billionaire Kroenke Gets Record Naming Rights Fee From SoFi." *Bloomberg Sports*, September 15, 2019. Blooberg.com (Accessed October 7, 2019)

on the home of the Rams and Chargers for the next two decades, but it will also have the naming rights on a stadium that will host the 2022 Super Bowl, the 2023 College Football Playoff National Championship, and the opening and closing ceremonies for the 2028 Olympic Games.

With all of those marketing dollars being invested in a sports and entertainment venue, SoFi must have a massive growth plan ahead for its company. So how might they get the most out of the sponsorship platform that is SoFi Stadium? In what ways could they apply Three-Win principles to ensure they become a beloved brand in the eyes of Rams, Chargers, and NFL fans? Let's make three recommendations for SoFi CEO Anthony Noto and his team.

1) **Intention**—In the press release announcing the sponsorship, the LA Rams and SoFi shared that, "community partnerships and programs will be announced in the coming months, leading up to the opening of the stadium."[84]

It seems as if the team and the brand have the best intentions in mind with respect to leveraging SoFi Stadium as a force for good in Inglewood and greater Los Angeles. However, between now and the opening of the stadium in the summer

---

84 Los Angeles Rams. "New Home Of The Los Angeles Rams Officially Named Sofi Stadium". TheRams.com, September 15, 2019. (Accessed October 7, 2019).

of 2020, it would behoove SoFi, the Rams, and the Chargers to lay out a clearly defined purpose for the social impact of this deal.

SoFi states on its website that its mission is to "help people achieve financial independence to realize their ambitions." Given how focused SoFi is on financial capability and independence, it seems to me it could leverage its stadium naming rights to undertake a massive financial literacy education campaign throughout greater Los Angeles.

Financial literacy is an important life skill for people of all ages and has been historically underemphasized in our school system. From NFL players down to elementary school students, everyone in Los Angeles could stand to benefit from educating themselves on the basics of personal finance.

Imagine SoFi launching a "SoFi Financial Scholars" community platform in which it brings financial literacy courses to Rams and Chargers players and to young people throughout LA Unified School District. SoFi could then work with both teams to run financial education workshops in which it brings NFL athletes and young people together to discuss and learn about banking, credit, saving for college, auto loans, and mortgages.

It would not require even close to twenty-five percent of the thirty million dollar-annual investment into SoFi Stadium to build an impactful financial literacy platform. Perhaps SoFi and its partners over at Kroenke Sports will take the time between now and summer 2020 to set the intention to improve the financial capability of all LA residents.

2) **Authenticity**—How might SoFi tell the story of its "SoFi Financial Scholars" platform in an authentic way that connects with its target markets? My suggestion would be to put a face to the stories, and I could see SoFi doing so in one of two ways.

First, if I were SoFi's sponsorship team, I would approach the Rams and Chargers searching for a player or a couple of players who have a genuine personal experience struggling with personal finances. That player could then be enlisted as a public face and spokesperson for the SoFi Financial Scholars platform.

The Rams or Chargers players could then record a video series, similar to the Kneading Dough series created by Uninterrupted and presented by Chase. Kneading Dough is hosted by LeBron James' business partner Maverick Carter and features real conversations about money with pro athletes and celebrities. SoFi might think about emulating that approach and tailoring the videos for both an adult audience and for young people so that the messaging is age-appropriate and easily digestible for all fans.

Alternatively, SoFi might enlist Rams and Chargers fans to submit their stories via video for an opportunity to be featured on SoFi's social media channels. Fans could be incentivized with a "SoFi Scholarship" for the best stories submitted. The scholarship could be put toward continued education for the winning fans or fans' children.

Ultimately, SoFi should think about emphasizing human stories about personal finance journeys. It will endear itself to fans not by highlighting the vast array of financial products it has to offer, but instead by telling the story of how the company empowers people to achieve financial independence.

3) **Ownership**—Here's where SoFi could get even more creative. In my mind, there would be a great opportunity to engage fans through social media with a simple hashtag that would trigger a donation from SoFi to an organization that supports the financial capability of all Los Angeles residents.

My suggestion here would be to take a page out of the T-Mobile #HR4HR playbook and attach a hashtag to a common play in an NFL game, such as a turnover or a sack. You could see a hashtag like #Sacks4Savings triggering a donation from SoFi every time a Rams or Chargers defender records a sack, plus fans on Twitter would trigger an additional, smaller donation each time they tweet #Sacks4Savings.

This social media strategy would give Los Angeles football fans the opportunity to celebrate a big defensive play in the game and feel great about supporting the financial well-being of themselves and their fellow fans. Most importantly for SoFi, it would be a great touch point with its target markets that would help consumers feel like they are part of something bigger than just a football game.

**

Brand leaders realize consumers are being bombarded with marketing and advertisements everywhere they go these days. So, as marketers, the question becomes "How do we stand out?" and "How do we cut through all of the noise to become a beloved brand?"

The answer is to stop talking about how great your brand is and to start talking about how big of a fan your brand is of your customer.

In the grand football game of the sports and entertainment industry, **brands should play the role of fans.** They are the cheerleaders for both the tremendous talent and teams throughout the industry and for the consumers they are so desperately trying to reach. To be successful in this new age of purpose-driven marketing, brands need to have a "we" not "me" attitude and approach.

THREE WINS FROM CHAPTER 11

- In the Three-Win sponsorship movement, brands play the role of **The Fans**. Sponsorship marketing for brands is all about integrating into fan bases and celebrating what players, teams, and fans have achieved together. Brands should not interrupt their target markets' experience at an event by communicating why their brand is so great. Instead, look to find common ground with target markets and add value to their experience.

- As Kim Skildum-Reid reminds us, the mission of sponsorship for brands is to "get on that unconscious list of brands that are loved and trusted by your target markets."

- SoFi Stadium, which opens in Inglewood, California, in summer 2020, will serve as a perfect opportunity for SoFi and its partners from the Rams and Chargers to implement Three-Win principles. My recommendation would be to invest in the financial capability of all Los Angeles residents and to get both players and fans engaged in learning the critical skill of managing personal finances.

CONCLUSION

—

"I really believe that we can be the generation that makes business better."

—ED FREEMAN

**

What is the purpose of business?

Leaders across the United States have debated this question for decades. In the late twentieth century, two voices emerged to answer this question.

In one corner was Milton Friedman, an economist and University of Chicago professor who won the Nobel Prize for Economics in 1976. Friedman published an essay in The New York Times Magazine in 1970 titled "The Social Responsibility Of Business Is to Increase Its Profits," which established his "shareholder theory."

Friedman's stance on the purpose of business was that "there is one and only one social responsibility of business—to use its resources and engage in activities designed to increase its profits so long as it stays within the rules of the game, which is to say, engages in open and free competition without deception or fraud."[85]

In the other corner was R. Edward Freeman, a professor of business administration at the Darden School of the University of Virginia. Freeman published a book in 1984 named *Strategic Management: A Stakeholder Approach*, in which he laid out his alternative: "stakeholder theory."

Freeman believed corporations must serve all "stakeholders," which he defined as "any group or individual who can affect, or is affected by, the achievement of a corporation's purpose." He felt Friedman's view on business was outdated and that "business is about purpose. Get the purpose right, and profits follow. It's about creating value for stakeholders,

---

85 Friedman, Milton. "The Social Responsibility of Business is to Increase its Profits." *The New York Times Magazine,* September 13, 1970. (Accessed via umich.edu on October 7, 2019).

not just shareholders. And it's about doing it without making trade-offs."[86]

By now, I am sure you can see which side of the shareholder theory vs. stakeholder theory debate I sit on. But what do the top business leaders in America think about this question? In summer 2019, we received an answer.

**

"The American dream is alive, but fraying," said Jamie Dimon, chairman and CEO of JPMorgan Chase & Co. and chairman of The Business Roundtable. "Major employers are investing in their workers and communities because they know it is the only way to be successful over the long term. These modernized principles reflect the business community's unwavering commitment to continue to push for an economy that serves all Americans."[87]

This statement, from the CEO of one of the largest financial institutions in the world, was included in an August 19, 2019, press release from The Business Roundtable. The Business

---

86 Freeman, R. Edward. *Strategic Management: A Stakeholder Approach.* Cambridge University Press, 2010.

87 The Business Roundtable. "Business Roundtable Redefines The Purpose Of A Corporation To Promote 'An Economy That Serves All Americans'". August 19, 2019. *Businessroundtable.Org.* (Accessed October 7, 2019).

Roundtable is "an association of chief executive officers of America's leading companies working to promote a thriving U.S. economy and expanded opportunity for all Americans through sound public policy."

In this press release, Business Roundtable members "redefined the purpose of the corporation to promote an economy that serves all Americans."

Up until this point, Business Roundtable had released a "Principles of Corporate Governance" document from time to time that subscribed to Milton Friedman's shareholder primacy theory. The new purpose statement, however, seemed to finally admit that Ed Freeman's stakeholder theory was right.

"While each of our individual companies serves its own corporate purpose, we share a fundamental commitment to all of our stakeholders," the statement read.

Among the stakeholders listed, Business Roundtable included customers, employees, suppliers, communities, and long-term shareholders.

"This new statement better reflects the way corporations can and should operate today," stated Alex Gorsky, CEO and chairman of the board of Johnson & Johnson and chair of the Business Roundtable Corporate Governance Committee. "It affirms the essential role corporations can play in improving our society when CEOs are truly committed to meeting the needs of all stakeholders."

"CEOs work to generate profits and return value to shareholders, but the best-run companies do more. They put the customer first and invest in their employees and communities. In the end, it's the most promising way to build long-term value," said Tricia Griffith, president and CEO of Progressive Corporation.

Business Roundtable's members sent a message validating Freeman's idea that we can "make business better." Is the sports and entertainment industry ready to answer the call?

**

The Business Roundtable story should give all players in the sports and entertainment industry the comfort and confidence to transform their businesses and adjust to this new era.

Business has evolved to be about something bigger than profits. It is time that we make every facet of our businesses about creating value for all of our stakeholders.

It is my hope that this book has given you inspiration to utilize the discipline of sponsorship marketing as a force for good. There are countless examples and templates out there of effective Three-Win deals that are creating value for society. It's time to begin internalizing those lessons and implement them into our work each and every day.

Sponsorship can be a powerful tool to make business better for all stakeholders. It can tell great stories. It can unlock resources to invest in communities. It can inspire and mobilize people to action.

My ask of you is to take action yourself. Take the lessons from this book and go do something. Call your partners and tell them about a great new idea you have for the sponsorship platform. Reach out to community organizations that you can partner with. Set up a meeting with leaders at your company and share a new vision for your sponsorship portfolio.

We can be the generation to make sponsorship better. Let's get to work!

APPENDIX

———

INTRODUCTION

IEG 2018. "What Sponsors Want & Where Dollars Will Go In 2018." Sponsorship.Com. (Accessed September 3, 2019). http://www.sponsorship.com/IEG/files/f3/f3cfac41-2983-49be-8df6-3546345e27de.pdf

Lynch Baldwin, Sarah and David Begnaud. "Hurricane Maria Caused An Estimated 2,975 Deaths In Puerto Rico, New Study Finds". Aug. 28, 2018. Cbsnews.Com. (Accessed September 3, 2019). https://www.cbsnews.com/news/hurricane-maria-death-toll-puerto-rico-2975-killed-by-storm-study-finds/

National Oceanic and Atmospheric Administration 2019. *Nhc.Noaa.Gov.* (Accessed September 3, 2019). https://www.nhc.noaa.gov/news/UpdatedCostliest.pdf.

T-Mobile, 2017. "T-Mobile Announces #HR4HR Home Runs For Hurricane Recovery". October 6, 2017. *T-Mobile.Com.* (Accessed September 3, 2019). https://www.t-mobile.com/news/hr4hr.

T-Mobile, 2018. "Following Florence, T-Mobile Brings Back #HR4HR, Home Runs For Hurricane Recovery, For MLB Postseason". 2018. *T-Mobile.Com.* (Accessed October 6, 2019). https://www.t-mobile.com/news/hr4hr-2018

CHAPTER 1

Badenhausen, Kurt. "How Arnold Palmer Earned $875 Million During Legendary Career In Golf." Forbes SportsMoney, September 26, 2019. (Accessed September 24, 2019). https://www.forbes.com/sites/kurtbadenhausen/2016/09/26/arnold-palmer-earned-875-million-during-legendary-career-in-golf/#6583ddb73e53

Davis, David. "Peter Ueberroth: Showing Us The Gold Standard | CSQ Magazine". 2017. *CSQ | Magazine, Events, Community.* (Accessed September 24, 2019). https://csq.com/2017/07/peter-ueberroth-gold-standard/

Futterman, Matthew. *Players: The Story of Sports and Money, and the Visionaries Who Fought to Create a Revolution.* Simon & Schuster, 2016.

Gelles, David. *"Golf Great Arnold Palmer Was Also a Pioneering Pitchman."* The New York Times, Sept. 26, 2016. (Accessed September 24, 2019). https://www.nytimes.com/2016/09/27/business/golf-great-arnold-palmer-was-also-a-pioneering-pitchman.html

Sandomir, Richard. *"Arnold Palmer and His Savvy Agent Set the Bar for Pitchmen."* The New York Times, Sept. 28, 2016. (Accessed September 24, 2019) https://www.nytimes.com/2016/09/29/sports/golf/arnold-palmer-mark-mccormack-advertising.html

Settimi, Christina. *"By The Numbers: The 2018 Pyeongchang Winter Olympics".* 2019. Forbes.Com. (Accessed September 24, 2019). https://www.forbes.com/sites/christinasettimi/2018/02/08/by-the-numbers-the-2018-pyeongchang-winter-olympics/#7a84742a7fb4.

Walker, Alissa. "How L.A.'s 1984 Summer Olympics Became the Most Successful Games Ever" *Gizmodo,* Feb. 6, 2014. (Accessed September 24, 2019). https://gizmodo.com/

how-l-a-s-1984-summer-olympics-became-the-most-success-1516228102

CHAPTER 2

Skildum-Reid, Kim. *The Corporate Sponsorship Toolkit: Using sponsorship to help people fall in love with your brand.* Freya Press, 2012.

CHAPTER 3

Bahr Thompson, Anne. *Do Good: Embracing Brand Citizenship to Fuel Both Purpose and Profit.* HarperCollins, 2017.

Deloitte Touche Tohmatsu Limited. "Millennials disappointed in business, unprepared for Industry 4.0." 2018 Deloitte Millennial Survey. (Accessed October 4, 2019). https://www2.deloitte.com/content/dam/Deloitte/global/Documents/About-Deloitte/gx-2018-millennial-survey-report.pdf

Gillette® 2019. "The Best Men Can Be." *Gillette.Com.* (Accessed September 30, 2019). https://gillette.com/en-us/about/the-best-men-can-be.

Keller, Valerie. "The Business Case for Purpose" 2014. *Hbr. Org.* (Accessed September 30, 2019). https://hbr.org/resources/pdfs/comm/ey/19392HBRReportEY.pdf.

Mull, Amanda. 2019. "Millennials Stare Into The Void, And Gillette Stares Back". *The Atlantic.* (Accessed September 30, 2019). https://www.theatlantic.com/health/archive/2019/01/gillette-ad-controversy/580666/#Correction.

Nielsen N.V. "Consumer-Goods' Brands That Demonstrate Commitment To Sustainability Outperform Those That Don't". 2015. *Nielsen.Com.* (Accessed September 30 2019) https://www.nielsen.com/us/en/press-releases/2015/consumer-goods-brands-that-demonstrate-commitment-to-sustainability-outperform/.

Zappulla, Antonio. "The Future Of Business? Purpose, Not Just Profit ". 2019. *World Economic Forum.* (Accessed September 30, 2019). https://www.weforum.org/agenda/2019/01/why-businesses-must-be-driven-by-purpose-as-well-as-profits/.

CHAPTER 4

Covey, Stephen. *The 7 Habits of Highly Effective People: Powerful Lessons in Personal Change.* Simon & Schuster, 2013.

Martin, Stephanie and Pat Gallagher. *Big Game Bigger Impact: How the Bay Area Redefined the Super Bowl Experience and the Lessons That Can Apply to Any Business.* Motivational Press, 2017.

CHAPTER 5

Avery, Jill, and Koen Pauwels. "Brand Activism: Nike and Colin Kaepernick." Harvard Business School Case 519-046, December 2018. Revised September 2019. (Accessed October 7, 2019) https://www.hbs.edu/faculty/Pages/item.aspx?num=55349

Charlotte Rail Trail (2019) "About — Charlotte Rail Trail". *CharlotteRailTrail*.org. (Accessed October 7, 2019).

Friend, Nick. "Just do it, Kaepernick and the NFL: Why Nike doesn't care about burning trainers," *SportsProLive*, September 6, 2018. (Accessed October 7, 2019). http://www.sportspromedia.com/analysis/just-do-it-kaepernick-nfl-nike-burning-trainers

Klein, David (2018). "Experts Weigh In: Was Nike's Colin Kaepernick ad a good idea?" *Marketing News,* (Accessed October 7, 2019) https://medium.com/ama-marketing-news/experts-weigh-in-was-nikes-colin-kaepernick-ad-a-good-idea-56bdf354e1d3

Linnane, Ciara (2018) "Nike's online sales jumped 31% after Kaepernick campaign, data show," *MarketWatch,* September 17, 2018 (Accessed October 7, 2019).

Nasdaq (2018) "Nike, Inc. Common Stock (NKE) Quote Summary and Data," *Nasdaq,* (Accessed October 7, 2019). https://www.nasdaq.com/market-activity/stocks/nke

Nike, Inc. (2018) "A Crazy Dream Becomes Reality When You Just Do It," *Nike.com,* (Accessed October 7, 2019). https://news.nike.com/featured_video/just-do-it-dream-crazy-film

Nike, Inc (2018) "Nike, Inc. (NKE) CEO Mark Parker on Q1 2019 Results – Earnings Call Transcript," *Seeking Alpha,* September 25, 2018 (Accessed October 7, 2019). https://seekingalpha.com/article/4208283-nike-inc-nke-ceo-mark-parker-q1-2019-results-earnings-call-transcript

Petrarca, Emilia. "What Nike's 'Just Do It' Slogan Means with Colin Kaepernick behind it," *The Cut,* September 5, 2018, (Accessed October 7, 2019) https://www.thecut.com/2018/09/nike-colin-kaepernick-ad-protests.html

Robinson, Charles (2018) "Colin Kaepernick's commercial is a big hit with consumers, according to industry group," *Yahoo Sports,* September 6, 2018. (Accessed October 7,

2019) https://sports.yahoo.com/colin-kaepernicks-ni-ke-commercial-big-hit-consumers-according-indus-try-group-035831547.html

Reuters (2018), "Nike's Kaepernick ad spurs spike in sold out items," *Business of Fashion*, September 19, 2018 (Accessed October 7, 2019). https://www.reuters.com/article/us-ni-ke-kaepernick/nikes-kaepernick-ad-spurs-spike-in-sold-out-items-idUSKCN1LZ2G4

U.S. Bancorp, 2019. "U.S. Bancorp 2018 Corporate Social Responsibility". *usbank.com*. (Accessed October 7, 2019). https://www.usbank.com/corporate-responsibility/annu-al-report/2018/index.html.

CHAPTER 6

Pac-12 (2018) "Launch Of 'Pac-12 Team Green' Announced". pac-12.com (Accessed October 7, 2019). https://pac-12.com/article/2018/07/12/launch-pac-12-team-green-announced

Pac-12 (2018) "Pac-12 And Unifi Announce Founding Partner-ship Of Pac-12 Team Green". (Accessed October 7, 2019). https://pac-12.com/article/2018/07/12/pac-12-and-unifi-announce-founding-partnership-pac-12-team-green

United Nations Framework Convention for Climate Change (2019) "Sports for Climate Action Framework," Unfcc.Int, (Accessed October 7, 2019) https://unfccc.int/climate-action/sectoral-engagement/sports-for-climate-action

UNFCCC, "Sports Launch Climate Action Framework At COP24". 2019. Unfccc.Int. (Accessed October 7, 2019) https://unfccc.int/news/sports-launch-climate-action-framework-at-cop24

University of Colorado Boulder (2016). "Water For The West". UC Boulder Environmental Center. colorado.edu/ecenter (Accessed October 7, 2019). https://www.colorado.edu/ecenter/greensports/water4west

CHAPTER 7

Anheuser-Busch InBev, Twitter Post, June 3, 2017, 8:35 AM. twitter.com/abinbev

Anheuser-Busch InBev. "2025 Sustainability Goals". 2019. *Ab-Inbev.Com*. (Accessed October 7, 2019). https://www.ab-inbev.com/sustainability/2025-sustainability-goals.html

Badenhausen, Kurt. "Anheuser-Busch Launches Revolutionary Incentive-Based Sponsorship Model". April 2, 2018.

Forbes.Com. (Accessed October 7, 2019). https://www.
forbes.com/sites/kurtbadenhausen/2018/04/02/anheus-
er-busch-launches-revolutionary-incentive-based-spon-
sorship-model/#27d19ba03d5f

Front Office Sports. "Shot Callers Episode 2: Nick Kelly, Head
Of US Sports Marketing, Anheuser-Busch Inbev". May
9, 2018. *frntofficesport.com.* (Accessed October 7, 2019).
https://frntofficesport.com/shot-callers-episode-2-nick-
kelly-head-of-us-sports-marketing-anheuser-busch-in-
bev/

IEG. "What Sponsors Want & Where Dollars Will Go In
2018." Sponsorship.Com. (Accessed September 3, 2019).
http://www.sponsorship.com/IEG/files/f3/f3cfac41-2983-
49be-8df6-3546345e27de.pdf

Lofton, Terry. "A-B'S Sponsor Shocker". April 2, 2018. *Sports-
businessdaily.Com.* (Accessed October 7, 2019). https://
www.sportsbusinessdaily.com/Journal/Issues/2018/04/02/
Marketing-and-Sponsorship/ABInBev.aspx

Skildum-Reid, Kim and Anne-Marie Grey. *The Sponsorship
Seeker's Toolkit, Fourth Edition.* McGraw Hill Education,
2014.

CHAPTER 8

Hellmann's® Canada. "Hellmann's® Feeds A Stadium Food Waste – Real Food Rescue". October 1, 2019. *Youtube.* (Accessed October 7, 2019). https://www.youtube.com/watch?v=hHsdI2sMihI

CHAPTER 9

BusinessWire. "LUNA® Bar Moves U.S. Women'S National Soccer Team One Step Closer To Equal Pay". *Businesswire. Com*, April 2, 2019. (Accessed October 7, 2019). https://www.businesswire.com/news/home/20190401005973/en/LUNA%C2%AE-Bar-Moves-U.S.-Women%E2%80%99s-National-Soccer

Das, Andrew. "U.S. Soccer Sponsor Enters Equal Pay Fight On Women's Side". 2019. *The New York Times,* July 14, 2019. *Nytimes.Com.* (Accessed October 7, 2019). https://www.nytimes.com/2019/07/14/sports/soccer/uswnt-equal-pay-ad.html

ESPN News Services. "USWNT suing U.S. Soccer for discrimination." ESPN.com, March 8, 2019. (Accessed October 7, 2019). https://www.espn.com/espnw/sports/story/_/id/26189867/uswnt-suing-us-soccer-discrimination

Evans, Morgan M. "Olympic Sprinter Allyson Felix Has a New Partnership That's Championing Female Athletes and Mothers" *PEOPLE*, July 31, 2019. people.com. (Accessed October 7, 2019). https://people.com/sports/allyson-felix/

Felix, Allyson. "Opinion: My Own Nike Pregnancy Story". *The New York Times,* May 22, 2019. *Nytimes.Com.*(Accessed October 7, 2019). https://www.nytimes.com/2019/05/22/opinion/allyson-felix-pregnancy-nike.html

Taylor, Charles. "Why The Allyson Felix And Athleta Partnership Will Work." *Forbes*, August 7, 2019. Forbes.com. (Accessed October 7, 2019). https://www.forbes.com/sites/charlesrtaylor/2019/08/07/allyson-felix-and-athleta-how-pregnancy-let-to-a-partnership/#6739fcca6abe

CHAPTER 10

Fischer, Ben and Terry Lofton. "Gold standard," *Sports Business Journal*, October 29, 2018. sportsbusinessdaily.com (Accessed October 7, 2019) https://www.sportsbusinessdaily.com/Journal/Issues/2018/10/29/In-Depth/LA28.aspx

CHAPTER 11

Los Angeles Rams. "New Home Of The Los Angeles Rams Officially Named Sofi Stadium". TheRams.com, September 15, 2019. (Accessed October 7, 2019). https://www.therams.com/news/new-home-of-the-los-angeles-rams-officially-named-sofi-stadium

Skildum-Reid, Kim. *The Corporate Sponsorship Toolkit: Using sponsorship to help people fall in love with your brand*. Freya Press, 2012.

Soshnick, Scott. "Billionaire Kroenke Gets Record Naming Rights Fee From SoFi." *Bloomberg Sports*, September 15, 2019. Blooberg.com (Accessed October 7, 2019) https://www.bloomberg.com/news/articles/2019-09-15/sofi-to-pay-30-million-a-year-for-la-rams-stadium-naming-rights

CONCLUSION

The Business Roundtable. "Business Roundtable Redefines The Purpose Of A Corporation To Promote 'An Economy That Serves All Americans'". August 19, 2019. *Businessroundtable.Org*. (Accessed October 7, 2019). https://www.businessroundtable.org/business-roundtable-redefines-the-purpose-of-a-corporation-to-promote-an-economy-that-serves-all-americans

Freeman, R. Edward. *Strategic Management: A Stakeholder Approach*. Cambridge University Press, 2010.

Friedman, Milton. "The Social Responsibility of Business is to Increase its Profits." *The New York Times Magazine,* September 13, 1970. (Accessed October 7, 2019). http://umich.edu/~thecore/doc/Friedman.pdf

ACKNOWLEDGEMENTS

—

3-Win Sponsorship would not have been possible without the incredible love and support of my family. Thank you to my parents, Cliff and Jane Balkam, for being my biggest fans and for giving me every opportunity to pursue my passions. Thank you to my older brothers—Matt, Andrew, and Jim—I've always looked up to you three and tried to emulate your best qualities. Thanks for not beating up on your little brother too bad when we were kids!

To Eric Koester—thank you for believing in my creative potential. Taking part in Creator Institute has transformed my life.

My publisher—New Degree Press—deserves a special thank you. Brian Bies and the whole team were so helpful and encouraging throughout this whole process. Thank you for everything!

Thank you so much to my editors—Jonathan Jordan, Ryan Palmer, and Katherine DeMatteo. You each brought something different to the table during this process and helped me improve my writing immensely.

I am deeply grateful for the individuals who agreed to be interviewed for this book. To Neill Duffy, Adam White, Ania Sponaski, Dave Newport, Marty Conway, Matt Mead, Malcolm Lemmons, Danielle Berman, Scott Tilton, Matt Hill, Sarah Stiles, and Matthew Campelli—thank you for your time and your thoughtful insights.

And thank you to everyone who pre-ordered the eBook, paperback, and multiple copies to make publishing possible! Thank you for spreading the word about *3-Win Sponsorship*, and helping me publish a book I am proud of. I am sincerely grateful for all of your help.

Amal Abukar

Jahan Addison

Kevin Anderson

Morgan Assel

Mary Austin

Michael Austin

Cliff Balkam*

Kyle Balkam

Emily Balkam

Molly Balkam

Erin Balkam

Andrew Balkam

Jane Balkam*
Matt Balkam*
James Balkam*
Kristen Bandos
Ian Barber
Michael Barnhart
Arrelious Benn*
Danielle Berman
Ramsey Brame
Tim Broughton
Troye Bullock
John Burns
Sophie Buzzell
Jon Chapman*
Michelle Chite
Ralph and Ruth Chite
Stephen Chite
Eileen Connors
Colm Cross
Emma Dickinson
Teresa Dickinson
Keegan Downey
Claire Duarte
Michael Evans
Faraaz Farooq
Jack Ferry
Elizabeth Figoni

Taylor Hanley
Tim Heard
Dennis and Perry Hooks*
Julia Hooks
Connor Hurson
Darian Johnson
Stephen Kae
Mackenzie Kaiser
Caroline Kay
Henry Kegan
Tracy Koczela
Julie and Jack Koczela
Luke Koczela
Eric Koester
Russell Kreutter
Richard Lafferty
Michael Ledecky
Chelsea Lee
Justin Leeson
Malcolm Lemmons
Jeremy Lent
Ellen and Bob Lent
Samantha Levitt
Dominic Liberatore
Bill McGoey
Mary Kate McTague
Joel Michaels

Jonathan Miller

David Mitchell

Luke Mohamed

Craig Montgomery

Fr. Ryan Muldoon

Madelyn Murphy

Andy Nelson

Mary O'Brien

Achal Patel

John Pfister*

William Potts

Mark Raza

Terry Redmond

Diego Regules*

Tyler Reiser

Chris Roche

Daniel Sabatano

Jesse Samuelson

Alexandra Santoli

Kushaan Shah

Aman Shahi

Colin Squier

Luke Stoiber

Ryan Swift

Sean Wallis

Daniel Wright

Chris Yedibalian

Andy Zipfel

* **Ordered multiple copies/made multiple campaign contributions**

Made in the USA
Columbia, SC
27 February 2022